Boulez
and the
Modern
Concept

Boulez and the Modern Concept

Peter F. Stacey

University of Nebraska Press

Lincoln

Published in England by Scolar Press
Published simultaneously in the United States
by the University of Nebraska Press

Library of Congress Cataloging-in-Publication Data

Stacey, Peter F.
  Boulez and the modern concept.

  "List of principal works": p.
  Bibliography: p.
  Includes index.
  1. Boulez, Pierre, 1925–
  —Criticism and interpretation.   I. Title.
ML410.B773S68   1987   780'.92'4   86–30818
ISBN 0–8032–4183–6

Contents

Preface

Pierre Boulez is generally acknowledged to be one of the most important figures in avant-garde music since the Second World War. Claude Samuel refers to him as 'the leading light of the new generation';[1] while Olivier Messiaen calls him, quite simply, 'a great composer'.[2] For a short period, in the rapidly changing world of new music, Boulez held a pre-eminent position in the avant-garde, attaining this position in the early fifties with his creation of a new musical language and syntax which drew on Webern's serial technique and Messiaen's rhythmic awareness. His music and new technique dominated the Darmstadt Summer School, which soon became a Mecca for aspiring composers. Although in the late fifties Boulez's position of predominance was threatened and overturned by the anarchic influence of John Cage, who led composers like Stockhausen away from the world of total serialism to that of music-theatre and chance-music, Boulez's achievement remains a considerable one. Not only do young composers still look to Boulez as a model but the compositions of his later period remain pieces of great stylistic purity, displaying his thorough compositional technique.

Bearing in mind Boulez's undoubted significance for twentieth-century music, it is rather surprising to find how little has been written on him, either as a man or as a composer. When I started this study, there was only one published monograph on Boulez, Antoine Goléa's *Rencontres avec Pierre Boulez* (Paris, 1958). Since that time, two books have appeared. Joan Peyser's 'psychobiography' of Boulez was published in Great Britain in 1977. This book, despite its dubious conception, is a mine of information, although the reader must beware, for some of its nuggets are fools' gold! More recently, Paul Griffiths's short analytical study has appeared. It focuses largely on the details of the development of Boulez's compositional technique and, despite its brevity, it makes many useful and valid points.

The difficulty of Boulez's music on every level – performance, analysis and aural appreciation – explains, to some extent, this dearth of literature. A composer who has a stated preference for 'work that resists easy comprehension' and can admire the poetry of Mallarmé for its 'density of texture' and 'obscurity of language'[3] is not likely to present the world with music that can be easily digested and quickly explained. Boulez has thrown down a challenge. His

1. Claude Samuel, *Panorama de l'art musical contemporain*, Paris, 1962, p 343.
2. Cited by Joan Peyser in *B.C.C.E.*, p 1.
3. *B.C.C.E.*, p 117.

music is difficult, his language can be densely textured and obscure, but those who rise to the challenge find that his music is rewarding and even awe-inspiring in its purity and singularity of purpose.

The aim of this book is to lay the groundwork for an appreciation of Boulez, to describe the aesthetic framework that underlies his compositional decisions. The study looks at Boulez's artistic *milieu* and examines his relationship to the painters, poets and musicians who were influential in the formation of his language and style. In considering Boulez's debt to artists of various disciplines, the discussion will be more or less exact and more or less analogous, depending on the discipline on which Boulez is drawing. In discussing the musicians on whom Boulez draws, direct comparisons can be made; in discussing the painters who have influenced him, however, comparisons can only be made by analogy. The discussion of literary forms allows both exact and analogous comparisons. Features of some literary forms can only be transposed into musical terms by analogy but, in the realm of poetry, where music and word may come into direct confrontation, precise comments can be made about the importance of that discipline for the composer.

Music is too often considered in isolation from other art forms. Indeed, it is a very different discipline from painting, for example, but this does not mean that the two forms are not related or that one cannot learn about one form by looking at the other. Boulez has been very much part of a modern movement, a movement which found expression through several different media. Boulez can be understood in terms of these extramusical disciplines and appreciation of his music can be heightened by the adoption of this perspective. Moreover, Boulez has a high estimation of the value of the contribution of extramusical disciplines for the creative musician. His attitude to extramusical disciplines is unique, many of his musical ideas being conceived in terms of painting, novel-writing or poetry.

However, it is poetry that has special significance for Boulez. Not only does he set to music the words of several poets, but poetic concepts form the basis of some of his instrumental pieces. Much of this study will focus on these poetically conceived pieces as well as his works for instruments and voices. Here, it will be possible to throw some light on Boulez's attitude to language, syntax, imagery, form and, indeed, communication, which is at the root of all artistic endeavour.

Acknowledgements

The present book is based on a study undertaken in the Music Department at the University of Liverpool. I would like to thank Dr Ian Williamson, who supervised the study so constructively; Professor Basil Smallman and Dr Robert Orledge, who read the text and made many valuable comments; and Professor Ian Bent of the University of Nottingham, whose critical remarks were most gratefully received. My thanks go also to Dr Denis Smalley of the University of East Anglia for his comments and advice.

In the course of the research, I became indebted to Dr Richard McGregor, who put his extensive knowledge of twentieth-century analytical techniques at my disposal; to my brother, Michael Stacey, who advised me on questions concerning both the painter's art and mathematics; to Dr Clive Scott, who helped with the translations of the poems; to Stephen Haynes and Peter Meilleur, who criticised my translations of Boulez's musicological writings; and to Christopher Fox with whom I had much stimulating and useful discussion. Nor would it have been possible for me to produce this book without the invaluable cooperation of the typists, Mrs Brooksbank, who worked on the initial study, and Judy Agar, who laboured through the subsequent revisions.

During the course of my research and the preparation of this book Pierre Boulez very kindly expressed his support for my work and readily consented to the reproduction of extracts from his compositions and writings. Grateful acknowledgements are also due to the following for permission to quote from the works cited:

Amphion/ United Music Publishers Ltd for the *Piano sonata no. 1* by Boulez; John Calder (Publishers) Ltd/ Editions du Seuil for *Notes of an apprenticeship* by Boulez; René Char for *Le marteau sans maître*; Reinhard Döhl for *Apfel*; Editions Durand/United Music Publishers Ltd for *Mode de valeurs et d'intensités*; Editions Gallimard for *Les matinaux* and *Fureur et mystère* by René Char, and *Face aux verrous* by Henri Michaux; Ernst Eulenberg Ltd for *Conversations with Célestin Deliège* by Boulez; Faber and Faber for *On music today* by Boulez and *Pedagogical sketch book* by Paul Klee; Eugen Gomringer for *Avenidas*; Granada Publishing Ltd for *birds (here, inven/* by e.e. cummings; Heugel et Cie for *Le visage nuptial* and *Le soleil de eaux* by Boulez; Peters Edition Ltd for *Aventures* by György Ligeti; Princeton University Press for *The*

Presence of René Char by M. A. Caws and *Poems of René Char* translated by M. A. Caws and J. Griffin; Schott & Co. Ltd for *Stimmen* by Hans Werner Henze and 'Ha Venido', *Canciones para Silvia* by Luigi Nono; Universal Edition (London) Ltd for *Circles*, *Laborintus II* and *Sequenza III* by Luciano Berio, *Cantata* by Harrison Birtwistle, *cummings ist der dichter, Don, Improvisation sur Mallarmé I, Improvisation sur Mallarmé II*, and *Le marteau sans maître* by Boulez, *Hymnen* and 'Music and Speech', *Die Reihe* 6 by Karlheinz Stockhausen; Universal Edition (Alfred A. Kalmus Ltd) for *Symphony* op. 21 by Anton von Webern; and Emmett Williams for *Cellar song*.

P F S
Cardiff 1986

In memory of my father, Frank Stacey
and
for my mother, Margaret

List of abbreviations

B.C.C.E.   J. Peyser, *Boulez: composer, conductor, enigma*, London, 1977

C.D.   P. Boulez, *Conversations with Célestin Deliège*, London, 1976

R.A.   P. Boulez, *Relevés d'apprenti*, ed. P. Thévenin, Paris, 1966. (This volume contains Boulez's essays on various aspects of music published between 1948 and 1962.)

O.M.T.   P. Boulez, *On music today*, tr. S. Bradshaw and R. R. Bennett, 2nd ed., London, 1975

I · The Basis of the New Aesthetic

...historians and aestheticians can, with just a few
strokes of the pen, connect everything with everything,
and anything with anything. This kind of subtle
reasoning is the basis of innumerable theses. Let's forget
the sophists!

Boulez, Darmstadt, 1960[1]

Boulez's warning is one that should be borne in mind by all musicologists who feel tempted to play the glass bead game. Bearing his admonition in mind and approaching the subject with all due circumspection, it is possible to connect Boulez with the names of a limited number of painters, poets, playwrights and musicians.

When Boulez entered the Paris Conservatoire in 1943 at the age of 17, he knew little of the key figures who were to be so important in the formation of his new aesthetic. However, in 1944 he entered Messiaen's harmony class and there was introduced to the music of Stravinsky; and in 1945 he attended one of Leibowitz's pioneering concerts of Schoenberg's music and commenced a period of study of the music of the Second Viennese School. His discovery of this new repertoire was 'very rapid' and many years later his preferences 'remain unchanged'.[2] He describes a similarly speedy process in the formation of his tastes in painting:

In 1945 and 1946 my preferences were really quite precise. . .not only in music but also in literature and painting.

The first time I saw paintings by Klee I was absolutely gripped by the force of his invention, and at that instant many other things fell to dust. It was in 1947, or perhaps slightly later, that I first saw paintings by Klee, Kandinsky and Mondrian; immediately I felt that here were three crucially important figures in the development of contemporary painting. Similarly my first encounters with Joyce, Kafka and – later – Musil made a real impression on me. I think I was fairly quick to define the world that preceded me, and this allowed me to make rapid progress because once the past has been got out of the way one need think only of oneself.[3]

If we can rely on the accuracy of Boulez's memory (and Boulez is certainly accurate in most other areas!), his contact with the new repertoire of music covers the years 1943–46 and his contact with

1. *O.M.T.*, p 14.
2. *C.D.*, p 35.
3. *C.D.*, p 36.

the painters took place around 1947. In a space of about four years, Boulez's tastes in music, painting and literature were clearly formed.

The impact of serial music and abstract art on post-war Paris

The formation of Boulez's new aesthetic seems to have taken place with the speed and fervour of a religious conversion. The appearance of Viennese atonal and serial music and German abstract art, in a Paris previously dominated by the neo-classicism of Nadia Boulanger and the various schools of painting which had not made a decisive break with representation, must, indeed, have seemed something of a revelation.

Although, in 1945, it was some thirty-three years since Schoenberg had composed *Pierrot lunaire*, and some twenty-four years since his invention of the twelve-note technique, France remained largely ignorant of the new atonal and serial styles. During the war years serial music had been suppressed as decadent and a manifestation of 'cultural bolshevism'. René Leibowitz, whose knowledge of the twelve-note technique ironically resulted from his private study of Schoenberg scores rather than from his studies with Schoenberg, was unable to publicise his discovery during the German occupation of France and had to wait for the liberation before he could begin to conduct concerts of Schoenberg's music.

It was one of Leibowitz's Schoenberg concerts in 1945 that had such a profound effect on Boulez. Significantly, it was the *Wind Quintet* op. 26, one of the early serial pieces of a most deliberate and cerebral construction, which was performed on this occasion. For a period of about one year, Boulez entered the tutelage of Leibowitz and during this period he encountered the works of Webern, which were to be so important to him.

Just as the revelation of the twelve-note technique was delayed by the German occupation of France and the Nazi régime's suppression of the modern movement, so was abstract art quashed in Germany. The effect of the Nazi régime on the development and spread of modern thought is one of the most interesting phenomena in the history of twentieth-century art. Germany and Austria were the homes of many of the more progressive modern schools. With the rise of the Nazis, many of the leaders of these movements either went into voluntary exile or were expelled. The arrival of such leaders in various European or North American centres influenced the development of movements which otherwise might have followed different courses. The Nazi attempt to suppress the progressive movements in Germany led, in the long run, to the dissemination of their thoughts and ideas in Europe and America.

The Bauhaus, the school founded by Walter Gropius in 1919 in the hope of creating a new style of contemporary architecture and industrial design, was closed by the Nazis in 1933. One result of the suppression of the school was the redistribution of its teachers. Two of the most important of these teachers were the Russian-born Wassily Kandinsky (1866–1944) and the Swiss, Paul Klee (1879–1940). Klee returned to Switzerland, but Kandinsky moved to Paris, where he lived, practically unknown, until his death. Shortly after his death, however, interest developed in his art and, in 1947, his work was revealed in a retrospective exhibition. Retrospectives, with their ability to present to the public an artist's work from early essays to maturity in a coherent manner, have often played important roles in art history and the development of style. Kandinsky's retrospective of 1947 was a prime example of this phenomenon. The impact of the new abstract style was sudden, changing the world of art in Paris swiftly and dramatically. A commercial gallery, exclusively for abstract art, was opened and the paintings of Paul Klee were exhibited for the first time. In the following years, exponents of the abstract style became numerous and many derivative styles appeared.

Pierre Boulez was a young man of twenty when the war ended. Exempt from military service, he had enrolled in the Paris Conservatoire and was ideally placed to absorb the new styles which were pervading that city. The two new styles, the twelve-note method and abstract art, had much in common: indeed, the movements were closely linked in the early days of expressionism. In 1912, the Blue Rider group published an almanac, *Der Blaue Reiter*, the purpose of which was to promote the new movement and emphasise the relationship between the arts. In this almanac, intended as the first of a series but the only issue to be published, a reproduction of Schoenberg's *Self Portrait* (1911) appeared alongside reproductions of his score of *Herzgewächse*, Webern's early song *Ihr tratet zu dem Herde*, and the first of Berg's three Mombert songs, Op. 2. Needless to say, reproductions of paintings by Kandinsky and Marc, the leaders of the group and editors of this almanac, were also included.

Both of the new styles were, in their own way, revolutionary, being involved in a break with long-established principles, music breaking with tonality and art with representation. Nevertheless, both can be seen as developments of trends in their respective fields. Schoenberg repeatedly insisted that his method was a natural extension of the Austro–German musical language of Brahms and Wagner, while the movements of Impressionism and Cubism had progressively eroded the pictorial element of painting, making a final break with representation inevitable. Boulez was, undoubt-edly, aware of the parallels between the two movements and seems to regard the painters' influence on him as of equal importance to that of the musicians for, when he is asked who the men are that have most influenced him, he inevitably mentions the names of Kandinsky and Klee in the same breath as the names of Webern and Schoenberg. Boulez's high regard for the value of the work of extramusical disciplines for the creative musician is reaffirmed by this comment on Debussy's music:

If one were determined to identify the sources of that modernity in music. . .it would probably be necessary to turn to the painters and poets whose influence was preponderant on the developing spirit of the young Debussy: Manet, Whistler, Verlaine. . .[4]

Kandinsky, Klee and Mondrian

In order to understand the importance for Boulez of the three progenitors of abstract and non-representational art, it is necessary to know something of the background and theoretical thought that underlie their work.

As one of the first painters of pure abstract works, Kandinsky was involved in a modern and pioneering capacity,[5] but the theory behind his pioneering effort was well grounded in nineteenth-century thought. Romantic philosophers regarded music as the greatest of the arts because of its remove from worldly subjects and its apparent ability to speak directly to the spirit. Friedrich Wilhelm Joseph von Schelling considered music as the art 'which to the greatest degree divests itself of corporeality and is borne upon invisible, almost spiritual wings'.[6] For Arthur Schopenhauer, the greatest virtue of music lay in its ability to speak directly to the 'Will' (the subjective self) without recourse to 'Ideas' (aspects of outer reality):

. . .music. . .entirely independent of the phenomenal world ignores it altogether, could to a certain extent exist if there was no world at all, which cannot be said of the other arts. . .Music is thus by no means like the *copy of the Will itself*. . .This is why the effect of music is so much more powerful and penetrating than the other arts, for they speak only of shadows, but it speaks of the thing itself.[7]

The Romantic belief in the superiority of music led to an effort by painters and poets to attain musicality in their respective media. Verlaine opened his poetic manifesto, *Art poétique*, with the words 'De la musique avant toute chose' ('Music before everything'). Verlaine did not mean simply that a poem should sound musical, but that it should aspire to the state of music, should aim to achieve its spiritual power of penetration.

Kandinsky expressed very similar ideas:

4. Pierre Boulez, 'La corruption dans les encensoirs', *R.A.*, p 37.
5. In the second decade of the twentieth century, pure abstract styles were being developed in Germany, Paris, Russia and Holland. In Paris, the heretic cubists, Robert Delaunay (1885–1941), Albert Gleizes (1881–1957) and Jacques Villon (1875–1963) went beyond the new abstract geometrical design of Picasso and Braque in a movement dubbed 'Orphism'. Also in Paris, Frantisek Kupka (1871–1957) and Hans Arp (1887–1966) independently developed abstract styles. However, the abstract movements in Paris remained little known and relatively unimportant. In Russia, Michael Larionov's (b 1881) 'Rayonist' movement explored purely abstract techniques. In the same country, the Suprematist movement, the prime exponent of which was Kazimir Malevich (1878–1935), developed styles of purely abstract geometrical design. In Holland, Piet Mondrian (1872–1944), Theo van Doesburg (1883–1931) and the De Stijl group expanded and explored the principles of Neo-Plasticism.

Deciding who painted the *first* abstract painting is not easy. There are two problems: first, one must decide which painting makes the most complete break with 'external reality' and so achieves the greatest abstract purity; and second, one must confirm the date of the painting. The problem of these combined subjective and objective decisions makes it impossible to resolve the question definitively.
6. Cited by Alfred Einstein, *Music in the Romantic era*, London, 1947, p 340.
7. Arthur Schopenhauer, *The world as will and idea*, vol. 1, tr. R. B. Haldane and J. Kemp, London, 1907, p 333.

FIGURE I

THE NEW · 5
AESTHETIC

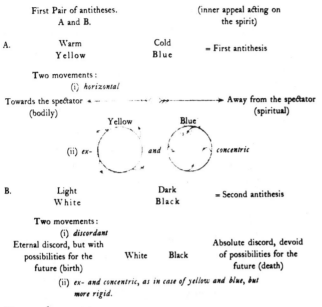

First Pair of antitheses.   (inner appeal acting on
    A and B.   the spirit)

A.   Warm   Cold   = First antithesis
      Yellow   Blue

    Two movements:
        (i) *horizontal*

Towards the spectator ← — — — — — → Away from the spectator
   (bodily)   (spiritual)

         Yellow   Blue

   (ii) *ex-*   *and*   *concentric*

B.   Light   Dark   = Second antithesis
      White   Black

    Two movements:
        (i) *discordant*
Eternal discord, but with   Absolute discord, devoid
  possibilities for the   White Black of possibilities for the
    future (birth)   future (death)

   (ii) *ex- and concentric, as in case of yellow and blue, but*
     more rigid.

Example 1

. . .there has never been a time when the arts approached each other more nearly than they do today. . .the various arts are drawing together. They are finding in Music the best teacher. With few exceptions music has been for some centuries the art which has devoted itself not to the reproduction of natural phenomena, but rather to the expression of the artist's soul, in musical sound.[8]

If music's great spiritual power results from its remove from the external world, from its fundamental autonomy, then painting must aspire to this state, or such was Kandinsky's contention:

A painter who finds no satisfaction in mere representation, however artistic, in his longing to express his inner life, cannot but envy the ease with which music, the most non-material of the arts today, achieves this end. He naturally seeks to apply the methods of music to his own art. And from this results that modern desire for rhythm in painting, for mathematical abstract construction, for repeated notes of colour, for setting colour in motion.[9]

In the chapter of *Concerning the spiritual in art* entitled 'The language of form and colour', Kandinsky attributed very specific meanings to these essential elements of his medium in order to create an artistic language which could exist without reference to external reality. He described the general characteristics of colours, often comparing them to the tone-colours of musical instruments, and classified them in terms of warmth or coldness, with an implied movement to, or away from, the spectator's spiritual self (Example 1). The theory of the technique of composition using only the basic components of the painter's art was further elaborated in

8. Wassily Kandinsky, *Concerning the spiritual in art*, New York, 1977, p 19. All quotations from *Concerning the spiritual in art* are taken from the Dover edition, which is an unabridged republication of the English translation first published, London, 1914, under the title *The art of spiritual harmony*.
9. Ibid.

Kandinsky's *Point and line in plane*, which was written in 1914 and published under the auspices of the Bauhaus in 1926.

Klee, like Kandinsky, had a fundamentally spiritual approach to art. Entries in his diaries reveal an attitude to the spiritual in art that is very close to that of Kandinsky:

One ascends the realm of the here and now to transfer one's activity into a realm of the yonder, where total affirmation is possible.
Abstraction.[10]

However, a more detailed examination of Klee's aesthetic theories reveals certain differences in the approach to the technique of abstraction. For Klee, art should not copy the actual manifestation of nature but should reproduce its *essence*: 'Art does not reproduce the visible, but makes visible'.[11]

Klee's technique was to start with an observation of nature and to reduce from this the basic laws 'to formulate a single, universal principle for the manifold, individual appearances of the splendid world garden'.[12] Through this process of observation, analysis and reduction, the artist achieves a heightened metaphysical view of the world. He becomes capable of forming 'free abstract structures which surpass schematic intention and achieve a new naturalness – the naturalness of the work. Then he creates a work, or participates in the creation of works that are the image of God's work.'[13] Like Kandinsky, Klee produced theories of working with the basic elements of the medium. Klee's *Pädagogisches Skizzenbuch* (Pedagogical Sketchbook), also published under the auspices of the Bauhaus, illustrates his technique of creating an artistic language based on principles of balance and movement observed in nature (Example 2).

Mondrian's Neo-Plastic theories, like the abstract theories of Kandinsky and Klee, also had a philosophical basis. Mondrian and Theo van Doesburg, two co-founders of the De Stijl group, were greatly influenced by the speculative mysticism of the philosopher–mathematician M.J.H. Schoenmaekers, who had a very specific influence in the development of the principles of Neo-Plasticism. It was he who observed:

The two fundamental, complete contraries which shape our earth and all that is of the earth, are: the horizontal line of power, that is the course of the earth around the sun, and the vertical, profoundly spatial movements of rays that originate in the centre of the sun.[14]

The principle of the opposition of vertical and horizontal was to become the basic principle of Mondrian's artistic technique.

Mondrian's Neo-Plastic laws, fundamentally derived from Schoenmaekers' observation of the vertical–horizontal duality of nature, were strict and uncompromising. In 1927, Mondrian had formulated five rules:

10. Cited in Christian Geelhaar, *Paul Klee and the Bauhaus*, Bath, 1973.
11. Ibid, p 25.
12. Ibid, p 26.
13. Ibid, p 27.
14. Cited in H. L. C. Jaffé, *De Stijl 1917–1931, The Dutch contribution to modern art*, Amsterdam, 1956, p 58.

(Symbol):

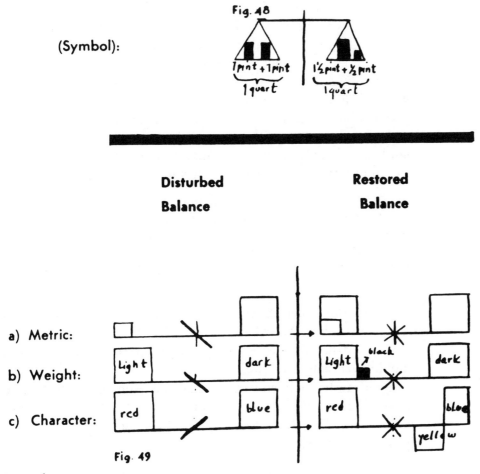

**Disturbed
Balance**

**Restored
Balance**

a) Metric:

b) Weight:

c) Character:

Fig. 49

Example 2

1 The plastic means must be the plane or the rectangular prism in primary colours (red, blue, yellow) and non-colour (white, black, grey). In architecture, empty space acts as non-colour and volume acts as colour.

2 The equivalence of the plastic means is necessary. Although differing in dimension and colour, they must nevertheless have the same value. Equilibrium generally requires a large area of non-colour and a similar area of colour or volume.

3 The duality of opposition in the plastic means is equally required in the composition.

4 Constant equilibrium is achieved through relationship of position and is expressed by the straight line (the limit of the plastic means) in its principal opposition.

5 Equilibrium neutralises and annihilates plastic means and is achieved through the relationships of proportion in which they are placed and which creates the living rhythm.[15]

The profound similarities between the three abstract artists who Boulez claims were influential in the formation of his aesthetic are easy to see, all three being motivated by a desire to portray a deeper spiritual reality through an abstract, autonomous, artistic language.

Not only were Kandinsky, Klee and Mondrian closely linked in their exploration of autonomous abstract art but they were also closely linked to the Second Viennese School and the development of twelve-tone composition.

Schoenberg's motivation in developing a new musical language carries many parallels with the development of the abstract painters' new languages. His writings on music express a spiritual orientation very akin to that of his counterparts in abstract art:

What really matters, the ability to listen to oneself, to look deep into oneself. . .instruction that is supposed to educate an artist could consist at most in helping him to listen to himself. Technique, the means of art, will not help him. This ought to be, wherever possible, occult knowledge, to which he alone has access who finds the way himself. He who listens to himself acquires this technique.[16]

Although this inner effort is for Schoenberg the most important requirement, he acknowledges that techniques should be learnt so that 'the artist will have the ability to accomplish whatever the spirit should eventually demand'.

Significantly, Schoenberg evokes the Romantic philosopher Schopenhauer in support of his ideas. Schoenberg's article published in *Der Blaue Reiter* quotes Schopenhauer's 'wonderful insight' into music:

The composer reveals the innermost essence of the world and pronounces the most profound wisdom in a language that his reason cannot understand. He is like a mesmerised somnambulist who reveals secrets about himself that he knows nothing about when he is awake.[17]

In the same essay, Schoenberg expresses his support for Kandinsky's spiritual effort of abstraction:

Kandinsky and Oskar Kokoschka paint pictures in which the external object is hardly more to them than a stimulus to improvise in colour and form and to express themselves as only the composer expressed himself previously. These are symptoms of a gradually spreading recognition of the true essence of art. And with great joy I read Kandinsky's book *Concerning the Spiritual in Art*, in which a way is shown for painters that arouses hope. . .[18]

While Schoenberg may be compared with Kandinsky, Webern may be compared with Klee. In his lectures collected under the title

15. Piet Mondrian in *De Stijl*, Jubilee Number 1927, pp 37–38, quoted in H. L. C. Jaffé, *De Stijl*, tr. R. R. Symmons and Mary Whittall, London, 1970.
16. Arnold Schoenberg, *Theory of harmony*, tr. Roy E. Carter, London, 1978, p 413.
17. Arnold Schoenberg, 'The relationship to the text', *Der Blaue Reiter*, tr. H. Falkenstein, London, 1974.
18. Ibid.

The path to the new music, Webern expresses an aesthetic attitude that is remarkably close to Klee's. Like Klee, Webern based his musical theories on the observation of nature: '...all art, and therefore music too, is based on rules of order, and our whole investigation of this material...can only aim at proving these rules to some extent.'[19] Webern uses Goethe's words as a statement of aesthetic objective: '...to get to know the laws according to which nature in general, in the particular form of human nature, tends to produce and does produce what she can...'[20] Webern, like Klee, believed that the artist's function was not to copy nature slavishly but to observe the essential qualities which operate in her and to use them to create a naturally defined aesthetic world. Art itself becomes a manifestation of nature: '...what we regard as and call a work of art is basically nothing but a product of nature in general.'[21] Webern's comment is very close to Klee's famous assertion that 'Art does not reproduce the visible, but makes visible' and his stated intention to achieve 'a new naturalness – the naturalness of the work'.

Webern's observations of the underlying principles of the natural sound world reveal striking parallels with Klee's observations. Compare the following comments on balance in the realm of music with Klee's ideas of balance in painting:

How did these scales (the Greek modes) come about? They are really a manifestation of the overtone series. As you know, the octave comes first, then the fifth, then in the next octave the third, and if you go on, the seventh. What is quite clear here? That the fifth is the first obtrusive note, that is to say it has the strongest affinity with the tonic. This implies that the latter note has the same relationship with the one a fifth lower. So here we have a kind of parallelogram of forces, 'equilibrium' is produced, there is a remarkable balance between forces pulling upwards and downwards. Now the remarkable thing is that the notes of Western music are a manifestation of the first notes of this parallelogram of forces: C(GE) – (DB) – F(CA). So the overtones of the three closely neighbouring and closely related notes contain the seven notes of the scale.

You see: as a material it accords completely with nature.[22]

To recapitulate, Boulez was influenced by a movement, in music and in the visual arts, which concerned itself with the expression of the 'inner' self, which aimed to achieve an abstract, autonomous status and, for this purpose, found it necessary to establish a new language. The movement was revolutionary, in that it overturned well-established principles, and traditional, in that its thinking drew so heavily on Romantic theories. The full significance of these features for Boulez becomes clear in the following chapters, where the discussion concerns Boulez's own attempt to create a new musical language, in an effort that was both revolutionary and traditionally based.

19. Anton Webern, *The path to the new music*, ed. Willi Reich, London, 1963, p 10.
20. Ibid.
21. Ibid.
22. Ibid, pp 12–13.

Webern, Schoenberg and Berg

The influence of a painter over a musician is one that takes place at a certain remove. However strongly a composer may be influenced by a painter, an effort of transposition remains; the painter's achievement must be given parallel musical terms before it can become part of the composer's work. Kandinsky, Klee and Mondrian contributed to the formation of Boulez's aesthetic at this remove but the contribution of the composers of the Second Viennese School was inevitably more direct and easily observable.

Although Boulez first made his acquaintance with the Second Viennese School through the music of Schoenberg, it is Webern whom he prizes most highly of the group. Boulez regards Webern as nothing less than the 'threshold'[23] and 'chief landmark'[24] of modern music. Webern attains this position in the eyes of Boulez through his foundation of a musical 'vocabulary' and 'indispensable musical grammar'.[25] The use of the terms 'vocabulary' and 'grammar' are slightly ambiguous in a musical context. One imagines that the term 'vocabulary' is used analogously to describe the cells of which a piece is made, that is, its intervals, and the term 'grammar' to describe the rules governing the use of these intervals. The intervals that are predominant in the works that Boulez holds in high regard are largely the intervals of the major seventh and the minor ninth, with the intervals of the tritone, the sixth, the minor seventh and the major ninth also playing a significant role. These intervals derive from the characteristic Webern series exhibiting strong internal thematic unity and being structured in four micro-series: groups of three notes containing a semitone and a third (Example 3). Webern's technique could be described as a technique of avoidance. All the intervals chosen avoid any reference to a tonal centre and the consistency with which Webern sustains this avoidance – his grammatical consistency – contributes to the purity of style that Boulez admires in him. These intervals, the basic terms of Webern's vocabulary, feature strongly in the music of Boulez, where they perform a similar role. Boulez, however, expands Webern's vocabulary somewhat, exaggerating octave displacements and using a greater variety of intervals (Examples 4 and 5).

In an article of 1957, Boulez elaborated on Webern's significance for modern music:

Certainly the most important phenomenon of our era, the threshold of contemporary music, in the sense that he has rethought the very notion of polyphonic music through the principles of serial writing (a writing which he discovered progressively in his works, through the primordial role he gives to the interval proper, and even to the isolated sound), such is Webern. Throughout Webern's work, one senses an effort to reduce the articulation of the discourse to serial *functions* as much as possible. For him, the purity and rigour of the experience were to be preserved above all.[26]

23. Cited in Joan Peyser, *B.C.C.E.*, p 82.
24. *O.M.T.*, p 19.
25. *C.D.*, p 17.
26. Pierre Boulez, 'Tendances de la musique récente', *R.A.*, pp 225–26.

The series of Webern's Concerto op. 24

Example 3

Example 4

I

Example 5. Boulez: *Piano sonata no. 1*

Boulez identifies three important features which have significance for modern music and, particularly, for his own style. The first of these is the fundamental rethinking of polyphony and the establishment of a new relationship between vertical and horizontal elements. Boulez implies that this new relationship is such as to make the traditional notions of vertical and horizontal redundant. This is a new style which cannot be explained in terms of traditional music ('the fundamental schemas of the preceding sound universe'). The creation of this new 'musical being' constitutes Webern's prime significance for Boulez. In making this assertion, Boulez would appear to be going against his more commonly expressed opinion, which emphasises the importance of Webern's vocabulary and grammar. However, Boulez does add that Webern's achievement was made possible by the importance that he placed on the interval and isolated sound – the vocabulary of the music.

The lesson Webern teaches of the possibilities of new relationships between vertical and horizontal elements is one well learnt by Boulez. However, Boulez goes beyond Webern. In his book containing the Darmstadt lectures, Boulez talks of vertical relationships functioning in three different ways, 'as basic material, as an intermediary factor in the elaboration of complex objects, or as a control in working with complex objects'. As Bayan Northcott has commented, the difficulty of this book 'springs from the nature of its terminology'.[27] The first category is simple enough: it describes the use of 'harmonic material' as an element in its own right. The second category describes the use of a vertical complex or 'harmony' to generate other 'harmonies'. The third category is an extension or inversion of the second: having 'elaborated complex objects' from a vertical complex, the complex can then be used to control and restrict the 'harmonies' generated. Horizontal or 'contrapuntal' relationships can also be divided into three categories: 'from point to point, from a group of points to another group of points, and finally the relationship between groups of groups'. The three categories of horizontal relationships which Boulez describes are more easily explained. The first category describes the combination of individual lines. The second category describes the combination of groups of lines: for example, one pair of lines may form a 'counterpoint' to another pair. The third category describes the juxtaposition of the groups described in category two (Example 6).

The second important feature that Boulez mentions – 'the articulation of the discourse [through] serial functions alone' – concerns the delineation of form through contrasts derived from the series, rather than through any other method. This feature also forms an important part of Boulez's style, and its operation is

Example 6

27. Bayan Northcott, 'Boulez's theory of composition', *Music and Musicians*, XX (1971), p 32.

described in detail in the analysis of *Bourreaux de solitude* in Chapter III.

Finally, the features of purity and rigour which Boulez admires in Webern are fundamental to Boulez's music; a rigorous application of predetermined, carefully thought-out plans, resulting in pieces of great stylistic purity.

A similarly uncompromising approach governs the orchestration in Webern's works, Boulez feels.

Orchestration no longer has a purely decorative function, but becomes part of the structure itself; it is a particularly effective means of relationship and synthesis of pitch, duration, and intensity. So much so that, with Webern, we can no longer talk of an evolved orchestration, but we must discover newly indispensable functions.[28]

Once more, this principle is adopted by Boulez and taken a step further with the serialisation of tone colour, a method Boulez describes in his article of 1952, 'Eventuellement. . .'. Another place where instrumentation helps to define form is in *Le marteau sans maître*, where each movement has a different instrumentation. (In this respect *Le marteau sans maître* is also indebted to Schoenberg's *Pierrot lunaire*.)

While the name of Webern seems to be most frequently on Boulez's lips, the contribution of the other members of the Second Viennese School should not be overlooked. *On music today* is a testimony to Boulez's sophisticated knowledge of the working techniques of all three composers and this knowledge is tributary to the development of his compositional technique.

Boulez classifies the three different approaches to serial composition and three different techniques of relating the general structures of the work to its generative structure (the series) in the following way:

1 Uniquity of the serial hierarchy; fixed typology and characterology (Schoenberg).

2 Uniquity of the series; selectivity due to the internal structural characteristics (Webern).

3 (One or more) multiform series of varying typology and characterology (Berg).[29]

Schoenberg's technique retains the integrity of the series, the whole work being based on only one 'generative structure', which retains its identity throughout the piece. Webern's technique involves the development of subgroups or privileged areas, unity being assured through the intrinsic relationship of subgroups to the series. Berg, however, achieves contrast, not within the series, but between series. Boulez sees the techniques of Webern and Berg as the most valuable. It is a mistake, he feels, to try to link all of a work to one 'central authority'. He feels it is necessary to develop sub-cate-

28. Pierre Boulez, 'Tendances de la musique récente', *R.A.*, p 228.
29. *O.M.T.*, p 103.

gories, to create systems of selection which develop from the original structure:

It would surely be illusory to try to link all the general structures of a work to one and the same global generative structure, from which they would necessarily derive in order to assure the cohesion and unity, as well as the uniquity of the work. This cohesion and uniquity cannot in my opinion be obtained so mechanically. . .[30]

This attitude to serial composition accounts for much of the difficulty encountered in analysing Boulez's work (see the analysis of *Bourreaux de solitude* in Chapter III).

Boulez's relationship to the three Viennese composers has undergone changes over the years. In an article of 1948, 'Incidences actuelles de Berg', Boulez attacked Berg for his attachment to tradition and his Romanticism:

Really, Berg is only the extreme point in a post-Wagnerian line, where the pleasant – in the most horripilating sense of the word – Viennese Waltz and the emphaticism of Italian *verismo* come to be equally mixed. . .One senses in Berg a disparate amalgam where the exoticism of the bazaar takes its place with the tango in the cantata *Der Wein*.[31]

In 1952, Boulez's uncompromising epitaph of Schoenberg announced 'Schoenberg est mort', and roundly condemned him:

We can reproach Schoenberg bitterly for this exploration in the realm of the dodecaphonic because it has been conducted perversely with such persistence. . .the confusion of theme and series in Schoenberg's serial works reveals quite clearly his inability to glimpse the sound world which the series invokes. Here dodecaphony consists only of a rigorous law for the control of chromatic writing. . .[32]

In more recent years, Boulez has come to admire the work of Berg and to admit its influence. In the early days, Boulez sought a vocabulary of modern music and it was to Webern that he had to turn, for Berg's and Schoenberg's vocabularies belonged so much to late Romantic tradition. Having established a vocabulary, this need being satisfied, Boulez discovered that:

. . .there was a lot more to Berg than his immediately accessible romanticism . . .what thrilled me as I went along was the complexity of his mind: the number of internal correspondences, the intricacy of his musical construction, the esoteric character of many of his references, the density of texture, that whole universe in perpetual motion. . .[33]

Boulez particularly admires Berg's sense of continuous development. He sees the ambiguity that results from Berg's ' "romanesque" or novel-like development' as a great virtue. Berg creates intricate forms 'which virtually never cease to develop and imply no return to earlier material'.[34] These forms repay repeated listenings and are open to many different 'levels of interpretation'.[35] Boulez

30. *O.M.T.*, p 99.
31. Pierre Boulez, 'Incidences actuelles de Berg', *R.A.*, p 237.
32. Pierre Boulez, 'Schoenberg est mort', *R.A.*, p 268.
33. *C.D.*, p 24.
34. *C.D.*, p 17.
35. *C.D.*, p 24.

feels that it is essential that a piece should be capable of interpretation on different levels.

A work whose course reveals itself completely at one hearing is flat and lacking in mystery. The mystery of a work resides precisely in its being valid at many different levels. Whether it be a book, a picture or a piece of music, these polyvalent levels of interpretation are fundamental to my conception of the work.[36]

Boulez's change in opinion, to some extent, redresses the balance in favour of Berg. Webern simply does not have Berg's quality of polyvalence:

Webern's work, once one has grasped its essence and vocabulary (and of course I am referring particularly to the last works), does not require a series of readings. It is like a picture by Mondrian. You can see its perfection and it is very striking, being stripped down to the absolute minimum – a truly austere kind of perfection; but when you see it again at a later date, it offers you nothing further. The next time I see the picture again it is the same – there aren't any different levels of interpretation.[37]

Unfortunately, Schoenberg is not the beneficiary of a similar reassessment. Recently, Boulez again criticised Schoenberg for his conservatism:

. . .instead of going forward he stuck to constant factors. Those rhythms of quite insufferable squareness, the diminishing level of invention (after 1920), the style, and finally the contrapuntal procedures which are academic and appear on every page.[38]

Boulez also criticises Schoenberg's neo-classicism in his adoption of 'dead forms' and the contradiction of forcing a new language into an outmoded form. Here, one imagines that Boulez is referring to works like the *Wind Quintet* op. 26, and other works of the twenties. Boulez feels that the musical invention is 'reshaped by the old forms to the point where it suffers and dries up'. Although Boulez criticises Schoenberg, the latter's music is not devoid of interest for him. He mentions Schoenberg's pianistic style as being influential in the formation of his own style of piano writing. He also admires the *Chamber Symphony* op. 9 for its continuous transformation of a single theme over four movements and Schoenberg's invention of a continuous form derived from symphonic movements.

It is important to see Boulez the polemicist 'in the round'. At various times in his career, he has been critical of his predecessors in serial composition, but it is understandable that a composer's attitude to the past should change as his compositional techniques develop and his needs alter. So it was with Boulez, as he championed first one then another member of the Second Viennese School. Each member of the group has contributed something to the development of Boulez's compositional technique and none can be ignored in a consideration of their importance for him.

36. *C.D.*, pp 24–25.
37. Ibid.
38. *C.D.*, p 30.

Messiaen and Stravinsky

It remains to consider the significance of two artists who were mentioned at the beginning of the chapter and whose importance is not accounted for by the Teutonic abstract / atonal invasion of Paris in 1945. The importance of Messiaen and Stravinsky, one a French national, the other a Russian exile who spent many years in France, resides in the area of rhythmic innovation and development – an area largely unexplored by the Viennese composers. Boulez came into contact with Messiaen at the Paris Conservatoire when he joined Messiaen's harmony class in 1944. Messiaen held advanced analysis classes for exceptional students outside the auspices of the Conservatoire, which did not afford Messiaen the status of Professor of Composition. In these classes, works of Stravinsky and of Messiaen himself were studied, and Boulez was led to an awareness that rhythm needed to be worked on for its own sake: 'After having analysed *The Rite of Spring* with him [Messiaen], or even his own works, I was convinced of the necessity of working at purely rhythmic invention.'[39] The importance of Stravinsky must be emphasised here for, although he represented many things that Boulez found objectionable in new music (particularly neo-classicism), his contribution plays an important part in the formation of Boulez's style. In 1948, Boulez described Stravinsky as 'the first person who consciously made an effort in the rhythmic sense'.[40]

The decisive step towards the serialisation of rhythm was taken, however, by Messiaen in his *Mode de valeurs et d'intensités*, which belongs to the *Études de rythme* (1949–50). Messiaen's invention of a modal technique of rhythm in *Mode de valeurs et d'intensités* resulted from his researches into rhythm and, particularly, his use of Indian rhythmic modes. Despite the fact that Boulez has criticised Messiaen's use of the rhythmic modes of other cultures, he was himself, nevertheless, influenced indirectly by them:

As you know, he [Messiaen] often makes use of rhythms drawn from either Greek or Indian music, and to my way of thinking that poses a problem. It is very difficult to introduce fragments of another civilisation into a work. This is what I believe now but I also believed it then; we have to invent our own rhythmic vocabulary in accordance with our own norms.[41]

The rhythmic modes of Messiaen's *Cantéyodjayâ* (1949) are the Indian *sharngadeva* rhythms. The application of a rigid rhythmic pattern of this sort provided an obvious model for the *Mode de valeurs et d'intensités*, where each note of a twelve-note mode is given a different rhythmic length in an ascending scale of either demi-semiquavers, semiquavers or quavers (Example 7). *Mode de valeurs et d'intensités* is significant for its approach to types of

39. *C.D.*, p 13.
40. Pierre Boulez, 'Propositions', *R.A.*, p 65.
41. *C.D.*, p 13.

Ce morceau utilise un mode de hauteurs (**36** sons), de valeurs (**24** durées), d'attaques (**12** attaques), et d'intensités (**7** nuances). Il est entièrement écrit dans le mode.

Attaques:

(avec l'attaque normale, sans signe, cela fait **12**.)

Intensités: *ppp* *pp* *p* *mf* *f* *ff* *fff*
1   2   3   4   5   6   7

Sons: Le mode se partage en **3** Divisions ou ensembles mélodiques de **12** sons, s'étendant chacun sur plusieurs octaves, et croisés entre eux. Tous les sons de même nom sont différents comme hauteur, comme valeur, et comme intensité.

Valeurs:

Division I: durées chromatiques de **1** à **12**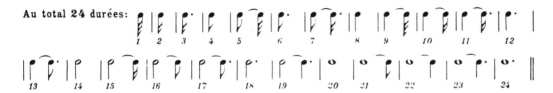

Division II: durées chromatiques de **1** à **12**

Division III: durées chromatiques de **1** à **12**

Au total **24** durées:

Voici le mode:

I

(la Division I est utilisée dans la portée supérieure du Piano)

II

(la Division II est utilisée dans la portée médiane du Piano)

III

(la Division III est utilisée dans la portée inférieure du Piano)

D. & F. 13.494

Example 7

42. Boulez was not the first to use the total serial technique, however. Milton Babbit published a theory of total serial composition in 1946, *The function of set structure in the twelve-tone system*, and put the theory into practice in his *Three compositions*, for piano, and the *Compositions for four instruments*, both of 1947. Nor was Boulez the only one of Messiaen's pupils to follow up the implications of *Mode de valeurs et d'intensités* and develop an integral serial technique. As Richard Toop points out in his interesting article 'Messiaen/Goeyvaerts, Faro/Stockhausen, Boulez', (*Perspectives of New Music*, Fall–Winter 1974, pp 141–69), the first phase of integral serialism is generally regarded as consisting of:

1 Messiaen's *Mode de valeurs et d'intensités* (1949)

2 Stockhausen's *Kreuzspiel* (1951)

3 Boulez's *Structures (premier livre)* (1951–52).

But this view ignores the contribution of two lesser-known composers, Karel Goeyvaerts and Michel Faro, who were also pupils of Messiaen. Toop suggests that Goeyvaert's Sonata for two pianos (1950–51) provided many important ideas for *Kreuzspiel*, and that Faro's Sonata (1951) may have provided a model for Boulez's *Structures, Livre I*.

attack and dynamics as well as rhythm: to each note is attributed one of twelve different degrees of attack and one of seven degrees of dynamics. The notes, being treated modally rather than serially, appear in any order, although the original note order is preserved at the outset.

The significance of Messiaen's and Stravinsky's innovations in the field of rhythm should not be underestimated. In Western music before this time, pitch was regarded as very much the dominant parameter, with rhythm taking a secondary role. Form was determined largely by pitch organisation: only in the isorhythmic works of the fourteenth and fifteenth centuries did rhythmic organisation play a determining role in the compositional process. It was in *Structures* of 1951–52 that Boulez first incorporated rhythm into the serial system.[42] His application and extension of the principles contained in Messiaen's crucial and catalytic piece are discussed in the analysis of *Bourreaux de solitude* in Chapter III. With the incorporation of Messiaen's rhythmic innovations into his serial technique, Boulez established the basis of his compositional technique.

Although his style was to undergo modification in later compositions, it remained, in many ways, closely related to the style he developed in this period. As Boulez has remained faithful to the artists who inspired the creation of his new aesthetic, so has he remained faithful to the basic style which was the result of his exposure to those artists.

II · Dramatic Influences

It seems that the present generation may take leave of its predecessors: it has come to define itself in a sufficiently precise and explicit way that it no longer needs fostering.

Boulez, 1954[1]

With the exception of Messiaen, the discussion of the opening chapter was concerned with artists who have influenced Boulez and who belong to the generation born in the eighteen-sixties, seventies and eighties. Discussion was further restricted to the two disciplines of painting and music. In this and subsequent chapters, however, the perspective is broadened to take into account artists who belong to the first decade of this century, as well as to Boulez's own generation. The discussion also includes consideration of the literary disciplines.

Asking Boulez about the men who have most influenced him, Joan Peyser repeatedly received this response: 'Klee, Kandinsky, Mondrian, Joyce, Char, Michaux, Artaud, Genet, Beckett, Messiaen, Webern – of course you know that – Schoenberg and Stockhausen'.[2] This list is surprising for several reasons. Although several of the figures included in it have already been discussed and their importance for Boulez cannot be questioned, some of the figures would appear to be of dubious significance for him. What is the exact significance of the playwrights Jean Genet (1910–86) and Samuel Beckett (b. 1906)? Boulez does not refer frequently, if at all, to them in his articles or recorded conversations.[3] They did not provide texts for him, as did René Char (b. 1907) and Henri Michaux (b. 1899), nor do they provide a conceptual basis for composition, as does Stéphane Mallarmé (1842–98).

If this list surprises us by the artists it includes, its omissions are no less astonishing. We have seen that, although Boulez was critical of Berg, he did see points of value in his music. Paul Cézanne (1839–1906), an artist whom Boulez himself compared to Berg,[4] and an important precursor of modern art, is also excluded. Franz Kafka

1. Pierre Boulez, '. . .Auprès et au loin', *R.A.*, p 183.
2. *B.C.C.E.*, p 177.
3. There is, however, a comment on Genet in *C.D.*, pp 37–38:

   I like people who are *self taught* – that is, those who have the strength of will to have done with models that existed before them. I might make a comparison with Genet's *The screens*. At a given moment the dead are represented as breaking through paper screens. I believe that to find one's true personality one has to break through screens of preceding composers.

4. *C.D.*, p 24.

(1883–1924) and Marcel Proust (1871–1922), important progenitors of modern literary trends, are excluded, despite the fact that Boulez speaks of them both with admiration. What, also, of Debussy, whom Antoine Goléa calls 'the starting point of the revolution in the musical language of our time'? Boulez is, on many occasions, prompted to write admiringly of his work, particularly his approach to tone colour, his use of suspended chords in a high register and his use of continuous form (in *Jeux*, for example). Debussy has also influenced the development of Boulez's literary and polemical style. The introduction to Boulez's Darmstadt lectures, called 'Interior Duologue', is clearly modelled on Debussy's introspective analysis, achieved with the aid of Monsieur Croche. Surely the most definitive statement of Boulez's high regard for Debussy is his entry in *Encyclopédie de la musique* (Fasquelle, 1958), which reads:

> . . .the flute of the *Faune* brings a new breath to musical art; the art of development is not overthrown there as much as the concept of form itself, liberated from the impersonal constraints of the diagram, releasing a supple and mobile expressivity, demanding a technique of perfect and instantaneous correspondence. The use of timbres seems essentially new, exceptional in its delicacy of touch. The use of certain instruments, flute, horn or harp, takes on the principal characteristics of the way in which Debussy used them in his later works; the writing for wind and brass, of an incomparable lightness of touch, constitutes a miracle of proportion, balance and transparency. This score contains a youthful potential which defies exhaustion and decay; in the same way that modern poetry surely takes its roots in certain poems of Baudelaire, it is justifiable to say that modern music awakes with *L'Après-midi d'un faune*.[5]

But the most astonishing exclusion from this list is the name of Stéphane Mallarmé, whose ideas were influential in several of Boulez's pieces and who forms the subject of the extended composition *Pli selon pli*, which is subtitled *portrait de Mallarmé*. An examination of the formative influences on Boulez cannot afford to ignore the nineteenth-century symbolist poet, such is his importance to Boulez. Although the other excluded figures have some significance for Boulez, their influence is only peripheral, not fundamental. In discussing Berg and Cézanne, Boulez said 'I am deliberately taking an example from a period that no longer concerns me',[6] which implies, perhaps, that those included in the list are only those who have a continuing influence over him. A more accurate explanation can be found for the exclusion of Kafka and other literary figures whom one might expect to be of importance to Boulez. In his article 'Son et verbe' of 1958, Boulez commented:

> One may note that the poets who have worked on language itself are those who leave the most visible imprint on the musician; the names of Mallarmé rather than Rimbaud, of Joyce rather than Kafka, come to mind.[7]

5. Pierre Boulez, 'Claude Debussy', *R.A.* p 336.
6. *C.D.*, p 24.
7. Pierre Boulez, 'Son et verbe', *R.A.*, p 58.

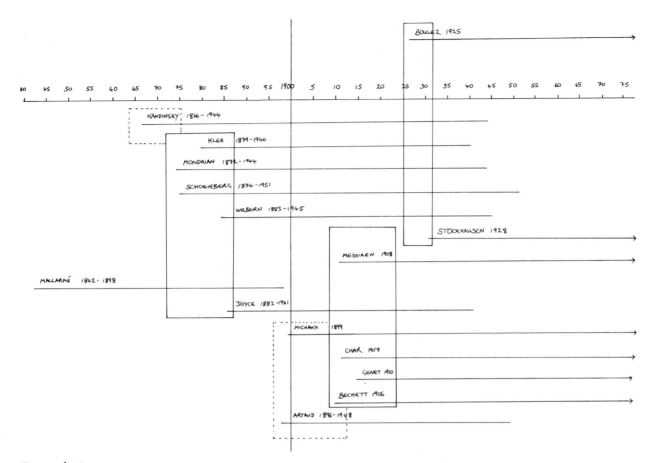

Example 8

On the date chart (Example 8), the lives of the artists influential upon Boulez have been plotted. Three groups of close contemporaneity emerge. The abstract painters Kandinsky, Klee and Mondrian belong to the same generation as Schoenberg and Webern. James Joyce (1882–1941) also belongs to this group. The dramatists Artaud, Genet and Beckett belong to the same generation as the poets Char and Michaux, and the composer Messiaen. Stockhausen belongs to the same generation as Boulez. Mallarmé falls well outside any of the generation groups, being the only one of the artists not to have seen the twentieth century. There are two generations, apart from his own, which have influenced Boulez. The first belongs to the eighteen-sixties, seventies and eighties. The second belongs to the last years of the nineteenth century and the first decade of the twentieth century.

While a graph of this nature is valuable to the musicologist, he must be critical in his use of it. Because Genet and Messiaen were born within two years of each other, one cannot assume that there

are, therefore, significant parallels between them. In fact, they are
very strongly contrasted: one was a criminal and an outcast, the
other a devout Catholic who held the post of organist at the Church
of the Holy Trinity. What does become clear is that these figures are
all linked by one feature, their rejection of traditional practices in
favour of new forms of expression.

Artaud, Genet and Beckett

For some of the figures mentioned above, rejection of tradition
meant only rejection of established principles within their own
disciplines. It is, perhaps, indicative of the nature of the
playwright's art that he should be involved in questioning not only
the conventions of his discipline but, also, the conventions of life
itself. The playwright, being involved in the depiction of life, is in a
position to question it and, for this reason, the theatre has the
greatest political potential of the arts. Although the writings of
Artaud have been used in recent years for political purposes, he was
not primarily a politician. Regarded by some as a prophet, detained
in a mental hospital for eight years, active as a film actor and theatre
director, Artaud has today become a symbol of revolution. In 1968,
French students printed his 'Lettre aux recteurs des universités
européennes', which read:

Europe crystallises and slowly mummifies under the chains of its frontiers, its
factories, its law courts, its universities. The frozen Spirit cracks under the slabs of
stone which press upon it. It's the fault of your mouldy systems, your logic of two
and two makes four, it is your fault, University Chancellors, caught in the net of
your own syllogisms. You produce engineers, judges, doctors unable to grasp the
true mysteries of the body, the cosmic laws of being, false scientists blind to the
world beyond the Earth, philosophers who pretend they can reconstruct the
Spirit. . .Leave us alone, gentlemen, you are nothing but usurpers. By what right
do you pretend to canalise intelligence, to award diplomas of the Spirit?[8]

This extract criticises established institutions on philosophical or
artistic rather than political grounds. If there was one consistent
strand in the turbulent life of the prophet–actor–poet Artaud, then
it was his feeling that the spirit of rationalism and analytical thought
was eating away at the fullness of man's emotional life and spiritual
awareness.

As Artaud was dissatisfied with the restrictive rational thought of
the West, so was he dissatisfied with the means of expression.
Artaud was not content with simply describing a feeling, he wanted
to communicate the feeling itself. During his involvement with the
Surrealist movement, Artaud tried to renew the power of language.
By applying a technique known as 'automatism', by breaking with
conventional forms of literature, and ignoring the rules of grammar
and aesthetics, Artaud hoped to let the subconscious speak directly.

8. Artaud, 'Lettre aux recteurs des
universités européennes', *La Révolution
Surréaliste*, iii (1925). Cited by Martin
Esslin, *Artaud*, London, 1976.

An awareness that an important part of thought was non-verbal caused Artaud to turn to the theatre, where his poetry could be given an extra-verbal dimension. The result of this train of thought was the 'Theatre of Cruelty' – a theatre where the audience would be involved in a complete experience – 'a crisis which is resolved either in death (!) or in the return to complete health'.[9] Ironically, the failure of Artaud's new theatrical theories and the period of severe disappointment which followed led to the creation of a poetic technique which realised his objectives and seemed capable of a direct expression of emotion.

Artaud presents a striking example of an artist who 'worked on language itself' and has, for that reason, been influential over Boulez. Indeed, Artaud has been a crucial figure in the development of Boulez's vocal style:

> The name of Artaud comes to mind immediately when one evokes questions of vocal emission or the dissociation of words and their fragmentation; actor and poet, he has naturally been attracted by the material problems of interpretation in the same way as a composer who plays or conducts. I am not qualified to study Antonin Artaud's language thoroughly but I can find again in his writings the fundamental preoccupations of modern music; hearing him read his own texts, accompanying them with cries, noises, rhythms, has shown us how to create a fusion of sound and word, how to make the phoneme spurt out when the word can do no more; briefly, how to organise delirium.[10]

Perhaps one of the texts accompanied with cries, noises and rhythms that Boulez may have heard was Artaud's radiophonic poem for four voices, xylophone and percussion, called *Pour en finir avec le jugement de Dieu* ('To have done with God's judgment'), which he prepared a short while before his death. Martin Esslin has described this recording as containing 'weird and violent words' and 'wild, piercing, inarticulate cries – outbursts of such intensity of anguish beyond speech that they freeze the blood'. Following Artaud's model of varied vocal emission with instrumental background, and Schoenberg's model of *Pierrot lunaire*, with its important new *Sprechgesang* technique, Boulez developed an individual method of voice treatment which included everything from singing *bouche fermée* to shouting. Boulez's treatment of the voice is discussed in detail in the following chapter.

Boulez's comment about the organisation of delirium brings us to another point of comparison between Artaud and Boulez. There is an interesting parallel between Artaud's 'automatic' technique, developed during his involvement with the Surrealist movement, and the technique adopted by Boulez at the outset of *Structures* of 1951–52:

> The first piece was written very rapidly, in a single night, because I wanted to use the potential of a given material to find out how far automatism in musical

9. Martin Esslin, *Artaud*, London, 1976, p 71.
10. Pierre Boulez, 'Son et verbe', *R.A.*, p 62.

Example 9

relationships would go, with individual invention appearing only in some really very simple forms of disposition – in the matter of densities for example. For this purpose I borrowed material from Messiaen's *Mode de valeurs et d'intensités*; thus I had material that I had not invented and for whose invention I deliberately rejected all responsibility in order to see just how far it was possible to go. I wrote down all the transpositions, as though it were a mechanical object which moved in every direction, and limited my role to the selection of registers – but even those were completely undifferentiated.[11]

Artaud and Boulez might also be compared in their seriousness of approach. There is something of the theatre of cruelty about Boulez's uncompromising *Structures Livre I*, which deals in extremes of every sort: extremes of dynamics from *ffff* to *pppp*; extremes of register; extremes of rhythmic complexity; and extremes of texture, from the single note melodic line to almost indecipherable note complexes (Example 9). Boulez perhaps comes closest to Artaud in his treatment of rhythm. In his article 'Propositions', Boulez comments: 'I think that music should be collective hysteria and enchantment, violently modern – following the direction of Antonin Artaud. . .'.[12] *Structures* is laden with such hysterical spells. The second piece is conceived as a contrast of moments of extreme activity with calmer passages:

…The second piece. . .consists of very long, static passages with almost no activity, alternating with active passages that are at first relatively complex and then amplified and superimposed on each other to produce extremely dense textures in which the listener will lose his way completely.[13]

Finally, Boulez shares something of Artaud's attitude to the establishment, although Boulez is a conformist by comparison. Compare these comments of Boulez on musical education with the extract from

11. *C.D.*, p 55.
12. Pierre Boulez, 'Propositions', *R.A.*, p 74.
13. *C.D.*, p 58.

...The whole system ought to be rethought...music education is clearly organised in accordance with absolutely mystifying and absurd norms. The teacher should not come with a completely dead curriculum referring only to the past...Everything finally comes to be seen in terms of examinations – a sort of police investigation into your ability to carry out one sort of work or another. That is why you see so many products of the music schools turning into dried fruit! – completely enclosed in a narrow conservatism and believing that because they found ways of existing in the music of the past they hold the key to truth.[14]

While Artaud and Boulez aim their polemics at the establishment largely when it encroaches on the vitality of the creative artist, Genet's attack on the establishment has a broader basis. Genet spent much of his early life in detention of some sort or another and was only released from a mandatory life sentence – which follows a tenth offence in France – following a petition signed by Jean-Paul Sartre and Jean Cocteau. Like Artaud, Genet does not spare the audience. *The Balcony*, for example, breaks down all vestiges of the respectability of establishment figures and finally challenges the audience to 'go home, where everything – you can be quite sure – will be even falser than here...'. Genet threatens our conception of reality and forces us into different levels of perception: this is where his significance for Boulez probably resides.

The bilingual playwright Samuel Beckett does not threaten the influence of the establishment over the creative artist, as does Artaud, nor does he question the social order, as does Genet. His attention is, instead, focused on philosophical conceptions. The style of drama Beckett developed has been called the 'Theatre of the Absurd' and is related to the Existentialist movement, which attempts to find meaning in the experience of nothingness and absurdity. Beckett is related to Artaud through the Existentialists,[15] who also believe that the institutions and systems of society, by overvaluing rational thought, have forced man out of his ontological awareness.

It is difficult to see exactly what Boulez takes from the absurd, existentialist world of Beckett. Something of the mood of Beckett's drama can be felt in the music of Boulez, however. The aimless wanderings of the alto flute in *Commentaire 1 de Bourreaux de solitude* and its accompaniment of sporadic percussive sounds (xylorimba with soft mallets; drum struck at the edges of the skin with light sticks; pizzicato viola with mute) combine to give a feeling of nothingness in their lack of purpose and direction (Example 9).

A comparison can, again, be made with *Structures*, where Boulez claims that he aimed for an effect of absurdity and disorder:

14. *C.D.*, pp 37–38.
15. Because of the confusion which surrounds the word 'existentialism', and the different meanings it has acquired, I include the following definition from Roger Fowler (ed.), *A dictionary of modern critical terms*:

Existentialism Literary and philosophical responses to the experience of nothingness and absurdity which attempt to discover meaning in and through this experience.

All existentialist writers start from a sense that an ontological dimension (Being; the Encompassing; Transcendence; the Thou) has been forced out of consciousness by the institutions and systems of a society which overvalues rationality, will-power, acquisitiveness, productivity and technological skill. Because this essential dimension properly constitutes the substantial unity between man and man, thing and thing, subject and object; and past, present and future, its loss is said to cause men to feel they have been thrown into a world of reified fragments which say nothing; into a world of men who talk past each other; and into a time-stream of disconnected present moments without past or future.

Although this definition is quite unlike the existentialism of the Christian, Kierkegaard, it holds good for post-war French writers like Sartre and Beckett.

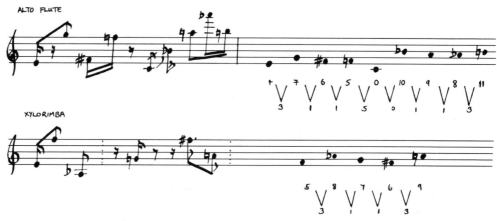

Example 10

I had taken the experience to absurd lengths, and it is very amusing that certain commentators, even those who are themselves composers, have failed to see this element of absurdity in the undertaking. I had made it perfectly clear from the start by choosing someone else's material. Thus this sort of absurdity, of chaos. . .tending almost towards the random, was completely intentional and has probably been one of my most fundamental experiments as a composer. At that point disorder is equivalent to an excess of order and an excess of order reverts to disorder. The general theme of this piece is really the ambiguity of a surfeit of order being equivalent to disorder.[16]

A similar relationship between order and disorder is found in Lucky's tirade in the first act of *Waiting for Godot*, where the excess of logic, the excess of learning, tends to absurdity:

Given the existence as uttered forth in the public works of Puncher and Wattmann of a personal God quaquaquaqua with white beard quaquaquaqua outside time without extension who from the heights of divine apathia divine athambia divine aphasia loves us dearly with some exceptions for reasons unknown but time will tell. . .

The purposeless world of *Godot* is strewn with symmetries which temper the absurdity and give it shape and proportion, if not meaning. Not only do speeches balance each other and acts maintain a symmetrical structure but individual phrases possess a symmetry the order of which is often a substitute for conventional meaning. The phrase 'the air the earth the sea the earth abode' from Lucky's tirade contains the approximate palindromic vowel sequence /ɛ/ /ð/ /ɪ/ /ð/ /o/, for example. A similar palindromic logic governs the interval relationships of *Commentaire 1 de Bourreaux de solitude*, the purposeless mood of which has already been compared to the existential nature of Beckett's plays.

16. *C.D.*, pp 56–57.

The interval sequence of the flute part in the sixth bar gives the approximate symmetry:

3, 1, 1, 5, 10, 1, 1, 3,

while the intervals of the xylorimba in bar eight read:

3, 11, 11, 3.

The intervals are considered as pitch class sets; that is, in close position attributing the numbers 0–12 to the ascending chromatic scale starting on C. The distance between intervals is calculated by subtraction (Example 10).

Covert symmetries of this sort achieve an effect directly comparable to Beckett's 'the air the earth the sea the earth...'

This is not to say that Boulez took *Godot* as a model, nor does it mean that he learned the palindromic technique from Beckett. It is more likely that he derives symmetries of this sort from Webern's models.

III · Poetic Confrontation I: the Char archipelago

If with painting the correspondences are necessarily
rather distant, it is different with poetry, the latter going
hand in hand with music, or at least, a domain of music
that relies on putting the vocal element into play.
Because, not to mention the theatrical context, music is
always confronting the word.

Boulez, 1958[1]

Boulez's relationship to poetry is one which is unique among composers. It could be compared, perhaps, to Messiaen's relationship to bird-song. Boulez describes poetry as 'a source of irrigation'[2] for his music. Not only does he set the words in the conventional manner but he looks to the poem to suggest the music's structure, from the smallest of details to the overall shape.

René Char: Le visage nuptial

The beginnings of Boulez's special relationship to poetry can be seen in his first setting of René Char's *Le visage nuptial* (1946–47). (The text of *Le visage nuptial* was first presented in a non-commercial, limited edition in 1938.) Boulez first discovered Char in the impressionable years following the war. He admired the qualities of concision, workmanship and violence in his poetry:

What struck me in Char's poetry when I first discovered it (in late 1945 or 1946) was, in the first place, its condensation. It was as if I had discovered a work of flint: it had a sort of contained violence – not a violence expressed in gestures, but an internal violence, concentrated in a very tense manner of expression. This was the first thing that struck me about him, and it still strikes me now. What I found most attractive about Char was not what people call his 'love of Nature', his feeling for Provence or direct relationship with humanity, but rather his power to sum up his world in an extremely concise form of expression, to exteriorise it and to fling it far away from him.[3]

Having read of Boulez's admiration of Char's 'concise form of expression', it is surprising to find that the text of *Le visage nuptial* is so very long. The cycle of poems on the poet's marriage are five in

1. Pierre Boulez, 'Son et verbe', *R.A.*, p 42.
2. Ibid, p 53.
3. *C.D.*, pp 43–44.

number, containing more than one hundred lines of verse. Despite the length, a high degree of concision and violence of expression is maintained. The poetry is enigmatic and the imagery obscure, but this is part of the poems' richness. As one might expect, the poems are laden with erotic imagery and, as Mary Ann Caws has pointed out, 'tragedy and cruelty are inseparable from Char's major love poems'.[4] Char's juxtaposition of seemingly contradictory feelings lends power to his verse:

4. M. A. Caws, *The presence of René Char*, Princeton, 1976, p 171.
5. Translation by M. A. Caws, ibid, p 171.

Tu vas nue, constellée d'échardes,	You go naked, studded with splinters
Secrète tiède et disponible,	Secret, warm and available,
Attachée au sol indolent,	Attached to the indolent earth,
Mais l'intime de l'homme abrupt dans sa prison.	But intimate to abrupt man in his prison.

In this verse from *Gravité* (Gravity), the second poem of the cycle, the conflict and violence of the imagery are most evident. The painful image *constellée d'échardes* is surrounded on each side by adjectives of warmth and availability. The conflict and tension between the lovers are probably expressed most concisely and poetically in this extract from Char's *Recherche de la base et du sommet* (Search for the base and the summit):

L'homme et la femme rapprochés par le resort de l'amour me font songer à la figure de la coque du navir lié par son amarre à la fascination du quai. Ce murmure, cette pesanteur flexible, ces morsures répétées, la proximité de l'abîme, et par-dessus tout, cette sûreté temporaire, trait d'union entre fureur et accalmie.

Man and woman brought together by the spring of love remind me of a boat's hull anchored to the fascination of the wharf. This murmur, this flexible weight, these repeated bitings, the proximity of the abyss, and above all, this temporary certainty, a joining between furore and calm.[5]

Le visage nuptial
par René Char

The nuptial countenance
by René Char

Conduite

Passage

Passe.
La bêche sidérale
autrefois là s'est engouffrée.
Ce soir un village d'oiseaux
très haut exulte et passe.

Pass.
The stellar spade
Was once swallowed up there.
This evening a village of birds
Passes over, high, exultant.

Écoute aux tempes rocheuses
des présences dispersées
le mot qui fera ton sommeil
chaud comme un arbre de septembre.

Listen at the rocky temples
Of the scattered spirits,
To the word that will make your sleep
As warm as a tree in September.

Vois bouger l'entrelacement
des certitudes arrivées
près de nous à leur quintessence,
ô ma Fourche, ma Soif anxieuse!

See the shifting network
Of certainties
Near us achieving their quintessence
Oh branch of my being, my anxious thirst!

La rigueur de vivre se rode
sans cesse à convoiter l'exil.
Par une fine pluie d'amande,
mêlée de liberté docile,
ta gardienne alchimie s'est produite,
ô Bien-aimée!

Life's rigours grind away
Relentlessly, coveting exile.
In a fine almond rain,
Mixed with docile freedom
Your guardian alchemy is manifest
Oh my beloved!

Gravité
L'emmuré

S'il respire il pense à l'encoche
Dans la tendre chaux confidente
Où ses mains du soir étendent ton corps.

Le laurier l'épuise,
La privation le consolide.

O toi, la monotone absente,
La fileuse de salpêtre,
Derrière des épaisseurs fixes
Une échelle sans âge déploie ton voile!

Tu vas nue, constellée d'échardes,
Secrète tiède et disponible,
Attachée au sol indolent,
Mais l'intime de l'homme abrupt dans sa prison.

A te mordre les jours grandissent,
Plus arides, plus imprenables que les nuages qui se
    déchirent au fond des os.

J'ai pesé de tout mon désir
Sur ta beauté matinale
Pour qu'elle éclate et se sauve.

L'ont suivie l'alcool sans rois-mages,
Le battement de ton triangle,
La main-d'oeuvre de tes yeux
Et le gravier debout sur l'algue.

Un parfum d'insolation
Protège ce qui va éclore.

Gravity
The immured one

If he breathes he thinks of the slit
In the soft confiding lime
Where his evening hands spread your body.

Laurel drains him,
Hardship strengthens him.

You, the monotonously absent one
Weaving saltpetre
Behind fixed thicknesses
An ageless ladder unfolds your veil!

You go naked, studded with splinters
Secret, warm and available,
Attached to the indolent earth,
But intimate to abrupt man in his prison.

The days grow having fed on you,
More arid, more impregnable than the clouds which are
    torn apart at the depth of your bones.

I have leant with all my desire
On your morning beauty
So that it may burst and escape.

Followed by alcohol without Magi
The throb of your triangle,
The labour of your eyes
And the gravel upright on the seaweed.

A perfume of insolation
Protects the coming blossom.

Le visage nuptial

À présent disparais, mon escorte, debout dans la
    distance;
La douceur du nombre vient de se détruire.

Congé à vous, mes alliés, mes violents, mes indices.
Tout vous entraîne, tristesse obséquieuse.
J'aime.

The nuptial countenance

Now, my escort standing in the distance,
    disappear;
The sweetness of number has just been destroyed.

Take leave, my allies, my violent ones, my indices.
Everything draws you away, obsequious sadness.
I love.

L'eau est lourde à un jour de la source.
La parcelle vermeille franchit ses lentes branches à ton
    front, dimension rassurée.
Et moi semblable à toi,
Avec la paille en fleur au bord du ciel criant
    ton nom,
J'abats les vestiges,
Atteint, sain de clarté.

Ceinture de vapeur, multitude assouplie, diviseurs de la
    crainte, touchez ma renaissance.
Parois de ma durée, je renonce à l'assistance de ma
    largeur vénielle;
Je boise l'expédient du gîte, j'entrave la primeur des
    survies.
Embrasé de solitude foraine,
J'évoque la nage sur l'ombre de sa Présence.

Le corps désert, hostile à son mélange, hier était revenu
    parlant noir.
Déclin, ne te ravise pas, tombe ta massue de transes,
    aigre sommeil.
Le décolleté diminue les ossements de ton exil, de ton
    escrime;
Tu rends fraîche la servitude qui se dévore le dos;
Risée de la nuit, arrête ce charroi lugubre
De voix vitreuses, de départs lapidés.

Tôt soustrait au flux des lésions inventives
(La pioche de l'aigle lance haut le sang évasé)
Sur un destin présent j'ai mené mes franchises
Vers l'azur multivalve, la granitique dissidence.

O voûte d'effusion sur la couronne de son ventre,
Murmure de dot noire!
O mouvement tari de sa diction!
Nativité, guidez les insoumis, qu'ils découvrent leur
    base,
L'amande croyable au lendemain neuf.
Le soir a fermé sa plaie de corsaire où voyageaient les
    fusées vagues parmi la peur soutenue
    des chiens.
Au passé les micas du deuil sur ton visage.

Vitre inextinguible: mon souffle affleurait déjà l'amitié
    de ta blessure,
Armait ta royauté inapparente.
Et des lèvres du brouillard descendit notre plaisir au
    seuil de dune, au toit d'acier.
La conscience augmentait l'appareil frémissant de ta
    permanence;
La simplicité fidèle s'étendit partout.

Water is heavy a day from its source.
The bright red particle clears its slow branches on your
    forehead, reassured dimension.
And I, like you,
With the flowering straw at the sky's edge shouting
    your name,
I, stricken, throw down the remains,
Healthy with light.

Sash of vapour, softened multitude, factors of fear,
    touch my renaissance.
Partitions of my duration, I renounce the help of my
    pardonable breadth;
I timber the device of the shelter, I shackle the first
    fruits of survivals.
Blazing with foreign solitude,
I imagine swimming on the shade of her Presence.

The desert body, opposed to mixture, yesterday had
    returned talking darkly.
Decline, do not change your mind, drop your club of
    fear, bitter sleep.
The neck-line diminishes the bones of your exile, of
    your swordplay;
You freshen slavery which eats its own back;
Night mockery, stop this dismal transport
Of glassy voices, lapidated departures.

Soon withdrawn from the flux of inventive injury
(The eagle's pickaxe throws high the flared blood)
On a present destiny I have led my frankness
Towards the multivalve blue, the dissident granite.

Oh vault of effusion on the crown of your belly,
Murmur of black dowry!
Oh desiccated movement of her diction!
Nativity, guide the unsubmissive, let them discover
    their base,
The almond credible in the new tomorrow.
The evening has closed its corsair's wound where empty
    rockets were travelling among the sustained fear of
    dogs.
Gone are the micas of grief in your face.

Inextinguishable windowpane: my breath was already
    flush with the friendship of your wound,
Arming your inconspicuous royalty.
Our pleasure descended from the lips of fog to the
    threshold of dune, to the roof of steel.
Consciousness increased to the trembling apparatus of
    your permanency;
Faithful simplicity extended everywhere.

Timbre de la devise matinale, morte-saison de l'étoile
    précoce,
Je cours au terme de mon cintre, colisée fossoyé.
Assez baisé le crin nubile des céréales:
La cardeuse, l'opiniâtre, nos confins la soumettent.
Assez maudit le hâvre des simulacres nuptiaux:
Je touche le fond d'un retour compact.

Ruisseaux, neume des morts anfractueux,
Vous qui suivez le ciel aride,
Mêlez votre acheminement aux orages de qui sut guérir
    de la désertion,
Donnant coutre vos études salubres.
 Au sein du toit le pain suffoque à porter
    coeur et lueur.
 Prends, ma Pensée, la fleur de ma main pénétrable,
Sens s'éveiller l'obscure plantation.

Je ne verrai pas tes flancs, ces essaims de faim, se
    dessécher, s'emplir de ronces;
Je ne verrai pas l'empuse te succéder dans
    ta serre;
Je ne verrai pas l'approche des baladins inquiéter le jour
    renaissant;
Je ne verrai pas la race de notre liberté servilement se
    suffire.

Chimères, nous sommes montés au plateau.
Le silex frissonnait sous les sarments de
    l'espace;
La parole, lasse de défoncer, buvait au débarcadère
    angélique.
Nulle farouche survivance:
L'horizon des routes jusqu'à l'afflux de rosée,
L'intime dénouement de l'irréparable.

Voici le sable mort, voici le corps sauvé:
La Femme respire, l'Homme se tient debout.

Évadné

L'été et notre vie étions d'un seul tenant
La campagne mangeait la couleur de ta jupe odorante
Avidité et contrainte s'étaient réconciliées
Le château de Maubec s'enfonçait dans l'argile
Bientôt s'effondrerait le roulis de sa lyre
La violence des plantes nous faisait vaciller
Un corbeau rameur sombre déviant de l'escadre
Sur le muet silex de midi écartelé
Accompagnait notre entente aux mouvements tendres
La faucille partout devait se reposer
Notre rareté commençait un règne
(Le vent insomnieux qui nous ride la paupière

Bell of the morning slogan, dead-season of the
    precocious star,
I come to the end of my arch, trenched Coliseum.
Enough of kissing the nubile horsehair of grain:
The carder, the obstinate, submits to our confines.
The haven of nuptial images is cursed enough:
I touch the bottom of a compact return.

Brooks, neume of the winding dead,
You that follow the arid sky,
Mix your journey with the storms of him who knew
    how to cure desertion,
In exchange for your salubrious studies,
In the bosom of the roof the bread suffocates to bring
    heart and light.
My Thought, take flower of my penetrable hand,
Feel the obscure plantation awaken.

I will not see your sides, these swarms of hunger, dry
    up filled with thorns;
I will not see the empuse succeed you in your
    greenhouse;
I will not see the buffoons' approach disturb the
    coming dawn;
I will not see the race of our liberty subserviently self-
    satisfied.

Chimeras, we have climbed to the plateau.
The flint was quivering under the twining stems of
    space;
Words, tired of beating, were drinking at the angelic
    wharf.
No savage survival:
The horizon of roads as far as the rise of the dews,
The intimate unfolding of the irreparable.

Here is the dead sand, here the saved body:
Woman breathes, Man stands upright.

Évadné

Summer and our life were one
The fields ate the colour of your fragrant skirt
Greed and constraint were reconciled
The Château de Maubec penetrated the clay
Soon the rolling of its lyre would break down
The violence of the plants made us vacillate
A crow, dark oarsman, leaving the squadron
On the mute flint of quartered noon
Accompanied our understanding with gentle movements
Everywhere the sickle had to rest
Our rarity was beginning a reign
(The sleepless wind wrinkles our eyelids

En tournant chaque nuit la page consentie
Veut que chaque part de toi que je retienne
Soit étendue à un pays d'âge affamé et de larmier
    géant)

C'était au début d'adorables années
La terre nous aimait un peu je me souviens.

Each night turning the agreed page
Wishing that each part of you that I retain
Be spread in a land of famished age and giant tear-
    ducts)

It was the beginning of the adorable years
The earth loved us a little I remember.

Post-scriptum

Écartez-vous de moi qui patiente sans bouche;
À vos pieds je suis né, mais vous m'avez perdu;
Mes feux ont trop précisé leur royaume;
Mon trésor a coulé contre votre billot.

Le désert comme asile au seul tison suave
Jamais ne m'a nommé, jamais ne m'a rendu.

Écartez-vous de moi qui patiente sans bouche:
Le trèfle de la passion est de fer dans ma main.

Dans la stupeur de l'air où s'ouvrent mes allées,
Le temps émondera peu à peu mon visage,
Comme un cheval sans fin dans un labour aigri.

Post-script

Leave me, in my mouthless waiting;
I was born at your feet, but you have lost me;
My fires have defined their kingdom too well;
My treasure has flowed against your block.

The desert as a refuge for the sole sweet firebrand
Has never named me, never surrendered me.

Leave me, in my mouthless waiting:
The clover of passion is iron in my hand.

In the air's stupor where my ways open,
Little by little time will trim my face,
Like an endless horse in its bitter ploughing.

Having sketched Boulez's emotional and intellectual relationship to Char and his cycle of poems on marriage, we can take into consideration some aspects of Boulez's setting of the poem and his attitude to the setting of poetry in general.

In the article quoted at the beginning of this chapter, Boulez expounded the problems of setting poetry to music:

When one envisages the 'musical setting' of the poem – staying outside the theatre – a series of questions arises concerning declamation and prosody. Is one going to sing the poem, 'recite' it, speak it? All the vocal means enter into play and the transmission, the more or less direct intelligibility of the text, depends on these diverse details of emission. It is clear that since Schoenberg and *Pierrot lunaire*, these problems have excited a great interest among musicians, and it is hardly necessary to recall the controversies *Sprechgesang* raised. As for that reflex response that one should have the sung poem scan like spoken poetry as closely as possible, now we can only find this to be a rather superficial kind of response. A good poem has its own sonorities when one recites it; it is useless to try to compete on this terrain with a medium that is perfectly balanced. If I sing a poem, I enter into a *convention*; it is more opportune to take advantage of this convention such as it is, with its specific laws, rather than to deliberately ignore it or want to dodge it and fake it in order to divert it from its true purpose. Song implies a transfer of the poem's sonorities onto intervals and into rhythms which differ fundamentally from spoken intervals and rhythms; it is not the heightening of diction, it is transmutation and, let us admit it, the displacement of the poem. Probably the poet will not at first recognise his text treated thus because he did not write it with this intention; even its sonorities will become strange and alien, because they are grafted onto an unforeseen support, not predicted by him; at best, and bearing in mind the poem's continuing autonomy, he will recognise that, if there was to be an intervention, it was necessarily this one. From this extremity of pure *convention* to that of spoken language itself, extends a very rich scale of intonations which we are only just beginning to exploit consciously. . .[6]

Recognising that a recitation of poetry over a musical background is an evasion of the issue and that conventional singing constitutes a destruction of poetry, Boulez began to explore 'that rich gamut of intonations' that separate the two extremes. In this exploration, conventional singing was taken as the base or starting point. *Le visage nuptial* constitutes his most extensive research into the possibilities, from singing *bouche fermée* to shouting.

In the opening pages of the score of *Le visage nuptial*, Boulez describes the various vocal techniques to be used under the heading 'Modifications de l'intonation vocale'. The various techniques, of course, require new symbols (Example 11). The first of these techniques is *intonation parlée à la hauteur indéterminée* (speech at an indeterminate pitch): the symbol shown in Example 11(a) is used for the various registers of the voice and for shouting. The second technique, *intonation parlée à la hauteur indiquée*, refers to speech at specific pitches (Example 11(b)). The third technique, *attaquer le son sur la hauteur exacte, puis transformer la voix en parlé (sans changer de hauteur)*, uses a symbol like Schoenberg's *Sprechgesang* symbol but it differs from that technique in that it asks the singer to start the note on an exact pitch before changing to speech style (Example 11(c)). The fourth technique, *presque chanté*, asks the singer 'almost' to sing and always to leave the pitch undefined (Example 11(d)). Microtonal singing can be justly considered as the fifth technique in the vocal gradation, its effect of off-pitch singing being some way between conventional singing and *presque chanté*. The microtonal system Boulez adopts introduces quarter-tones between each of the semi-tones (Example 11(e)). Boulez comments that *la notation habituelle est réservée à l'intonation chantée* (conventional notation is reserved for sung intonation): this could be regarded as the sixth category. Another type of vocal production that Boulez uses, but does not mention in the introductory pages, is singing *bouche fermée*, which constitutes the seventh and final category. In addition to these techniques, Boulez uses the word *Sprechstimme* itself in the opening of *Le visage nuptial*.

Boulez has, himself, commented on the importance of Schoenberg in the formation of these varied styles of vocal emission. Characteristically, Boulez extends Schoenberg's practice, providing seven techniques where, before, there was one.[7] Boulez's extended techniques sometimes lead to puzzling contradictions. How, for example, does one move from song to speech *without*

6. Pierre Boulez, 'Son et verbe', *R.A.*, pp 58–59.
7. Strictly speaking, Schoenberg uses more than one style of vocal emission. In *Pierrot lunaire*, for example, he occasionally asks for words to be whispered, sung without tone (marked *tonlos*), or sung in the normal way. However, these techniques occur rarely and do not threaten the predominant vocal style of *Sprechstimme*. Schoenberg does not aim for a large scale contrast of vocal styles but simply to highlight one or two words in the text.

Example 11: a, b, c, d & e

transforming the pitch? Surely the most significant difference between speech and song resides in the control of pitch. One assumes that in this category Boulez is inviting the singer to produce a voice that resembles the spoken voice and to eschew the refinements and techniques of the trained singing voice. The difference between this category and conventional singing is best explained as a rather subtle modification of the tone quality of the singing voice. As a whole the seven techniques form a spectrum extending from speech to song, progressively abandoning the defining characteristics of speech to arrive at the purely musical extreme of wordless song.

Boulez's application of these techniques must be seen in the broader terms of the structure of the music, their function being not merely colouristic but formal. To quote again from Boulez's 'Son et verbe':

. . .if there must be a connection between poetry and music, it is to this notion of structure that one will appeal most effectively, and I mean from the basic morphological structures to the most vast defining structures. If I choose a poem to make something other than the point of departure for an ornamentation that will weave arabesques around it, if I choose the poem in order to install a source of irrigation for my music and to create from this an amalgam so that the poem finds itself 'centre and absence' of the sonorous body, then, I cannot limit myself only to the affective relations which these two entities maintain; thus, a tissue of conjunctions imposes itself which comprises, among other things, the affective relations, but also covers all the poem's mechanisms, from pure sonority to intelligent ordering.[8]

Some of the ideas here mentioned are more applicable to *Le marteau sans maître*, particularly the concept of 'centre and absence', which will be discussed later. The first feature connecting music and poetry, however, the concept of structure 'from the basic morphological structures to the most vast defining structures', can be easily observed in *Le visage nuptial*.

Taking the macrostructure first, one obvious but valid point can be made. The five poems of the cycle are treated in five separate movements, thus observing the shape of the cycle. Moreover, the five movements are differentiated by their style of vocal treatment. The first movement, *Conduite*, is largely sung, but has a limited use of the third vocal technique described above (song–speech). The second movement, *Gravité*, is dominated by microtonal singing but also makes use of the second technique (speech at pitch) and the devices of *glissando* and *bouche fermée* chorus. The central poem of the cycle, *Le visage nuptial*, has a mixture of all the techniques but is dominated in its closing stages by the fourth vocal technique (imprecise singing) and the third technique (song–speech). The fourth movement, *Évadné*, is entirely spoken, the speech type adopted being that found in the first category (speech without pitch). The fifth movement, *Post-scriptum*, combines the first and fifth techniques (speech without pitch and microtonal singing). To summarise, the definition of the movements by predominant vocal style appears as follows:

1 *Conduite*   sung
2 *Gravité*   microtonal singing
3 *Le visage nuptial*   a mixture
4 *Évadné*   speech without pitch
5 *Post-scriptum*   microtonal singing and speech without pitch.

The central poem of the cycle, the longest movement of the work, has the most varied vocal treatment, taking elements from all the outer movements. This asserts its dominance and central position not only in the sequence of movements but in the meaning of the

8. Pierre Boulez, 'Son et verbe', *R.A.*, p 58.

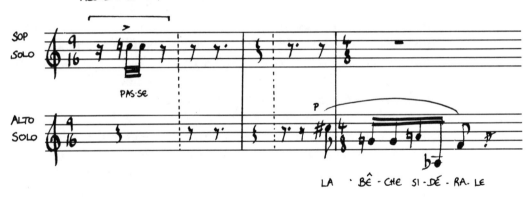

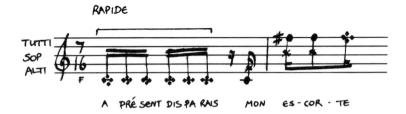

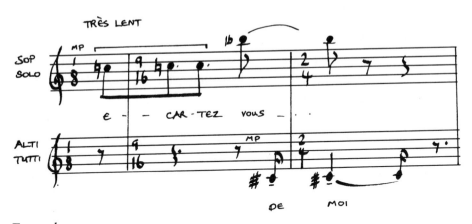

Example 12

cycle. Movements 1, 2 and 4 are distinguished by more or less exclusive use of one technique, while *Post-scriptum* superimposes the microtonal technique of the second movement over the speech without pitch of the fourth.

Boulez's awareness of the structure of the poems and his desire to translate that structure into musical terms is seen, also, in his use of a short motif that relates the important imperatives of movement that occur at the beginning of the first, third and final poems. The three directives, *Passe* (Pass on); *À présent disparais, mon escorte* (Now disappear, my escort); and *Écartez-vous de moi* (Leave me), can be interpreted as orders to the poet's companions, *mes alliés, mes violents* (my allies, my violent ones) to leave him on his wedding night, as *La douceur du nombre vient de se détruire* (The sweetness of number has just been destroyed).[9] The three imperatives of movement are unified by being set to monotones in short, isolated, rhythmically even groups (Example 12). The last two directives are highlighted by being set unaccompanied, whilst the first is reinforced by wind, string and percussion tones.

In examining the use of vocal techniques to define the macrostructure of the cycle, it was necessary to make generalisations and simplifications. In the following consideration of the smaller details, or microstructure, a more detailed examination of the use of the various techniques for expressive or 'affective' purposes will be made. Boulez uses the widest palette of vocal colour available and he does not fail to realise its expressive potential. In the opening stanzas of the central poem, for example, the poet asks his companions to leave him and gives the simple explanation – *J'aime*. Mary Ann Caws has commented on the impact of this line:

The poet speaks his love in the simplest and briefest way; the verb in its monosyllabic strength devoid of qualifier and even of object. Yet the sentence is complete, as the formulation is sufficient. 'J'aime'. In its wide context the word stands out sharply. . .[10]

Boulez shows his awareness of the power of this line by setting it to the longest melisma, in a setting which is largely syllabic because of the great length of the text. Moreover, the melisma is sung in the conventional way and so is differentiated from the first lines, which are spoken or in *Sprechstimme* (Example 13).

Another opportunity for word-painting presents itself in the third stanza of the same poem, the fourth line reading: *Avec la paille en fleur au bord du ciel criant ton nom* (With the flowering straw at the sky's edge shouting your name). Boulez avoids the obvious and does not set the word *criant* with a shout but preserves the sung intonation and provides a *glissando* on the words *ton nom*, the last of which is marked *étouffé* (stifled). The effect is infinitely more subtle (Example 14). Many examples of the expressive use of varied modes of vocal emission can be found. The entire setting is characterised by an acute sensitivity to the relationship of words and music. One of the most dramatic uses of vocal effects must be the setting of the second occurrence of the line *Écartez-vous de moi*, where the chorus first speaks the words *à mi-voix sans nuance* (in half voice

9. See the opening two stanzas of the central poem of the cycle, *Le visage nuptial*.
10. M. A. Caws, op. cit, p 176.

Example 13

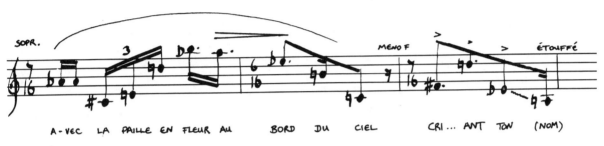

Example 14

without overtones) and then *fort-haché et violent* (very staccato and violent). Significantly, this is the only place in the text where word repetition is used. The vehemence of expression is complemented by its austere percussion accompaniment (Example 15).

Boulez's sensitivity to the French language is as evident in his setting of individual words and phrases as in his 'intelligent ordering' of those phrases. Just as he observed the division of the poems, making five separate movements out of the five poems of the cycle, so does he observe the division of stanzas within each poem. Stanzas are separated by short pauses in the singing, longer pauses occurring where a break in the logic of the poem requires it. For example, a short break in the singing occurs between the second and third stanzas of *Gravité*, where the text changes from description to direct speech. The contrast is reinforced by the removal of the *bouche fermée* chorus which has accompanied the soloists up to that point (Example 16).

Example 15

Example 16

René Char: Le soleil des eaux

Boulez's second setting of poems by René Char was started in 1948 and later revised in 1950 and 1958 and again in 1965. His composition and revisions of it therefore overlapped with the composition and revision of *Le visage nuptial*.

Le soleil des eaux is a setting of two poems by René Char: *Complainte du lézard amoureux* from the group of poems entitled *La sieste blanche* published in the collection *Les matinaux* (1950), and *La Sorgue: chanson pour Yvonne* from *La fontaine narrative* which appeared in *Fureur et mystère* (1948). Boulez gives his setting the title of Char's play that was first presented as a radio drama and for which Boulez provided incidental music. The drama was politically motivated, not intended as high literature, but written in the language of day-to-day conversation. It treats of the revolt of the fishermen of the river Sorgue, whose livelihood and life style was threatened by industrial pollution of the waters. The two poems have no place in the drama itself, but are concerned with related subjects. *Complainte du lézard amoureux* is about the natural environment and man's relationship to it. It describes an equilibrium of man and nature – the very thing that pollution would disrupt. *La Sorgue: chanson pour Yvonne* is obviously about the river that is at the centre of the drama, but it is equally concerned with the play's dedicatee, Yvonne Zervos, a longtime friend of Char.

Beyond their relationship with the central themes of Char's drama, the poems carry a great depth of meaning. Moreover, they acquire particular significance through their juxtaposition. *Complainte du lézard amoureux* is as much a love poem as a poem about nature: it describes love as a state of complacent resignation. By contrast, *La Sorgue: chanson pour Yvonne* describes a state of independence, violent and forward moving, a lonely condition but one that permits idealism in its 'respect for dreams'. *La Sorgue* presents an image of strength in a 'world crazy for prison'.

A quotation from the opening of *Les matinaux*, from which *Complainte du lézard amoureux* is drawn, is inserted by Boulez at the head of the score. Herein lies a clue to the significance of these texts for him:

11. The musicologist must beware of trying to apply definite dates to the works of a composer who continually revises his works. Boulez himself has commented: 'Je vis dans une éspace de plasma qui me permet de me déplacer en glissant d'avant en arrière. J'irradie dans plusiers directions à la fois. Je ne me détache jamais entièrement d'une oeuvre.' (I live in an area of plasma which allows me to slide forward or backward. I radiate in several directions at once. I never detach myself from a work.) Cited in Jean-Pierre Derrien, 'Dossier: Pierre Boulez', *Musique en Jeu*, i (1970), 109.

Nous avons sur notre versant tempéré une suite de
chansons qui nous flanquent, ailes de communication
entre notre souffle reposé et nos fièvres les plus fortes.
Pièces presques banales, d'un coloris clément, d'un
contour arriéré, dont le tissu cependant porte une
minuscule plaie. Il est loisible à chacun de fixer une
origine et un terme à cette rougeur contestable.

We have within us on our temperate slope a series of
songs which accompany us, wings connecting our
relaxed breathing to our highest fevers. Pieces almost
banal, mild in their colouring, recessed in their contour,
whose fabric bears nevertheless a tiny wound. Anyone
may set an origin and an end to this questionable
redness.[12]

Complainte du lézard amoureux

N'égraine pas le tournesol,
Tes cyprès auraient de la peine.
Chardonneret, reprends ton vol
Et reviens à ton nid de laine.

Tu n'es pas un caillou du ciel
Pour que le vent te tienne quitte,
Oiseau rural: l'arc-en-ciel
S'unifie dans la marguerite.

L'homme fusille, cache-toi:
Le tournesol est son complice.
Seules les herbes sont pour toi,
Les herbes des champs qui se plissent.

Le serpent ne te connaît pas,
Et la sauterelle est bougonne;
La taupe, elle, n'y voit pas;
Le papillon ne hait personne.

L'écho de ce pays est sûr.
J'observe, je suis bon prophète;
Je vois tout de mon petit mur,
Même tituber la chouette.

Il est midi, chardonneret.
Le séneçon est là qui brille.
Attarde-toi, va, sans danger:
L'homme est rentré dans sa famille!

Qui, mieux qu'un lézard amoureux
Peut dire les secrets terrestres?
Ô léger gentil roi des cieux,
Que n'as-tu ton nid dans ma pierre!

Lament of the lizard in love

Do not pick at the sunflower's seeds.
Your cypress trees would be distressed.
Goldfinch, fly again
And return to your woollen nest.

You are not a pebble of the sky
For the wind to hold you, to leave you
Rural bird: the rainbow
Is unified in the daisy.

Man is out shooting, hide:
The sunflower is his accomplice.
Only the grasses are with you,
The pliant field grasses.

The snake does not know you,
And the grasshopper is grumbling;
The mole, she sees nothing;
The butterfly hates no one.

The echo of this land is true.
I watch, I am a good prophet;
I see everything from my little wall,
Even the owl's lurching.

It is midday, goldfinch.
The groundsel lies shining there.
Take your time, go, without danger:
Man has gone home to his family!

Who better than a lizard in love
Can tell the secrets of the earth?
Oh light and gentle king of the skies,
Why isn't your nest in my rock!

12. René Char: *Poems of René Char*, tr.
M. A. Caws and J. Griffin, Princeton,
1976, pp. 120–21.

La Sorgue: chanson pour Yvonne

Rivière trop tôt partie, d'une traite, sans
    compagnon,
Donne aux enfants de mon pays le visage de ta passion.

Rivière où l'éclair finit et où commence ma
    maison,
Qui roule aux marches d'oubli la rocaille
    de ma raison.

Rivière, en toi terre est frisson, soleil anxiété.
Que chaque pauvre dans sa nuit fasse son pain de ta
    moisson.

Rivière souvent punie, rivière à l'abandon.

Rivière des apprentis à la calleuse condition,
Il n'est vent qui ne fléchisse à la crête de
    tes sillons.

Rivière de l'âme vide, de la guenille et du soupçon,
Du vieux malheur qui se dévide, de l'ormeau, de la
    compassion.

Rivière des farfelus, des fiévreux, des équarrisseurs,
Du soleil lâchant sa charrue pour s'acoquiner au
    menteur.

Rivière des meilleurs que soi, rivière des brouillards
    éclos,
De la lampe qui désaltère l'angoisse autour de son
    chapeau.

Rivière des égards au songe, rivière qui rouille le fer,
Où les étoiles ont cette ombre qu'elles refusent
    à la mer.

Rivière des pouvoirs transmis et du cri embouquant les
    eaux,
De l'ouragan qui mord la vigne et annonce le vin
    nouveau.

Rivière au coeur jamais détruit dans ce monde fou de
    prison,
Garde-nous violent et ami des abeilles de l'horizon.

The Sorgue: song for Yvonne

River setting forth too soon, at one bound, without a
    companion,
Give the children of my land the face of your passion.

River where the lightning finishes and where my home
    begins,
Which rolls the rubble of my reason to the steps of
    forgetfulness.

River, in you the earth is a shiver, the sun anxiety.
Let each poor man in his night make his bread of your
    harvest.

River often punished, river neglected.

River of apprentices in callous condition,
There is no wind that does not bend at the crest of
    your furrows.

River of the empty soul, of rags and suspicion,
Of ancient misfortune unwinding itself, of the elm tree,
    of compassion.

River of the crazy, of the feverish, of knackers,
Of the sun leaving the plough to descend to the
    liar.

River of those better than oneself, river of blooming
    mists,
Of the lamp which quenches anguish around
    its brim.

River of respect for dreams, river which rusts iron,
Where the stars cast that shadow that they refuse to the
    sea.

River of transmitted powers and of the cry of
    navigating the waters,
Of the hurricane which tears at the vine and announces
    the new wine.

River with a heart never destroyed in this world crazy
    for prison,
Keep us violent and friends of the bees of the horizon.

The various techniques of vocal emission play a large part in the characterisation of the poems. The techniques employed are the same as those in *Le visage nuptial*, with the exception of microtonal singing, which is not used. *Complainte du lézard amoureux*, for soprano solo and orchestra, is dominated by the vocal techniques of conventional singing, imprecise singing and song–speech. There is very occasional recourse to speech at pitch and there are only two melismas. This means that the vocal styles employed belong to the middle ground of available techniques. By contrast, *La Sorgue* opens with the two extremes, *bouche fermée* singing and speech at pitch, and then proceeds to explore the full range of intonations. Moreover, *La Sorgue* introduces male voices and grouped voices for the first time. In this way, Boulez uses the varied techniques of vocal emission and the interplay of male and female voices to define in musical terms the contrast between the two poems.

In *Complainte du lézard amoureux*, we see the first glimmerings of Boulez's technique of contrasting poetic and musical forms. *Complainte du lézard amoureux* consists of successive sections of orchestral and unaccompanied vocal writing. Only one stanza in the poem, the second, is sung to an orchestral accompaniment. The patterns resulting from the interplay of orchestra and voice create a musical form that, in some ways, reinforces the poetic form and, in others, creates an independent musical form not suggested by the poem.

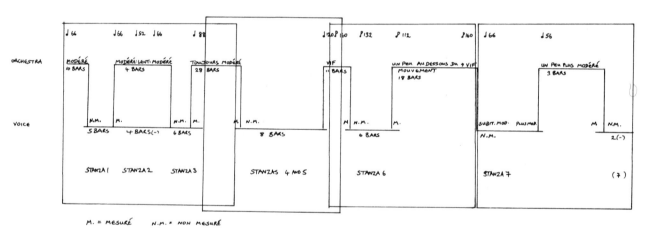

Example 17

Boulez treats the seven stanzas of the poem in four formal groups. The first contains stanzas one, two and three; the second contains stanzas four and five; the third contains stanza six; and the fourth contains stanza seven. The first group creates a symmetrical form, opening and closing with orchestral passages (Example 17). At the centre of this group is the only passage in the movement in which the voice is accompanied by the orchestra and has to sing in 'measured' rhythm. Notice, also, that the symmetrical pattern of interplay of voice and orchestra is reinforced by the choice of tempo. The music moves from moderate tempo through a central slow section and returns again to moderate tempo. The second

Example 18

formal group contains stanzas four and five which are both sung unaccompanied. The third group consists of stanza six, sung unaccompanied, and flanked by two sections in fast tempo. The last group reverses the pattern of the third, an orchestral passage being enclosed by two passages for solo voice.

There was certainly some justification in treating the first three stanzas as a formal group, for these stanzas tend to the imperative mood: *N'égraine pas le tournesol* (Do not pick at the sunflower's seeds); *cache-toi* (hide). Moreover, they contain the warning to the goldfinch of the coming of Man. Stanzas four and five, the second formal group, are linked through their descriptive mood (here one understands that the goldfinch has obeyed the imperatives of the opening stanzas and *is* hiding from Man). Stanza six, the third group, returns to imperative mood as the goldfinch is told:

Attarde-toi, va, sans danger:	Take your time, go, without danger:
L'homme est rentré dans sa famille!	Man has gone home to his family!

The final stanza, the fourth group, is rhetorical in nature and is thus clearly distinguished from its predecessors. In this way, it can be seen that Boulez's treatment of the text elucidates the structure and meaning of the poem.

The use of tempo in the creation of form is also of interest. In the diagram (Example 17), it will be seen that, although most of the music is in moderate tempo, the third group uses fast tempos, creating heightened tension at this point. The form observes the principle of climax at or near the golden mean, a formal principle common in most Western music. It is hard to see any justification in the text for the placing of the climax at this point. Here, the musical logic could be said to be functioning independently of the poetic logic.

The curve form described by the tempo succession is reinforced by the pitch organisation. The movement opens with the twelve-note series in prime order, aggregated in the orchestral part and in linear form in the vocal part (Examples 18, 19), and ends with the series in retrograde of prime order. The idea of opening and closing with the series in prime order and its retrograde, whilst having its own laudable musical logic, may also have been suggested by the text – the goldfinch, his disturbance and his return to peace. In this respect, the musical form accords with the poetic form.

Whilst the musical form of *Complainte du lézard amoureux* in some ways reinforces the poetic form and in other ways departs from it, the musical structure of *La Sorgue*, the second movement, follows most clearly the form of the poem. The poem consists of ten couplets and one stanza of only one line. Each stanza opens with the word *Rivière*. To translate the structure into musical terms, Boulez

Example 19

uses two variables, modification of vocal emission, and contrast of groups and solo voices. Either contrast is made between the couplets, successive couplets being set in one predominant vocal style or vocal configuration, or a modification is made within the stanza which is then contradicted at the start of the next stanza (Example 20).

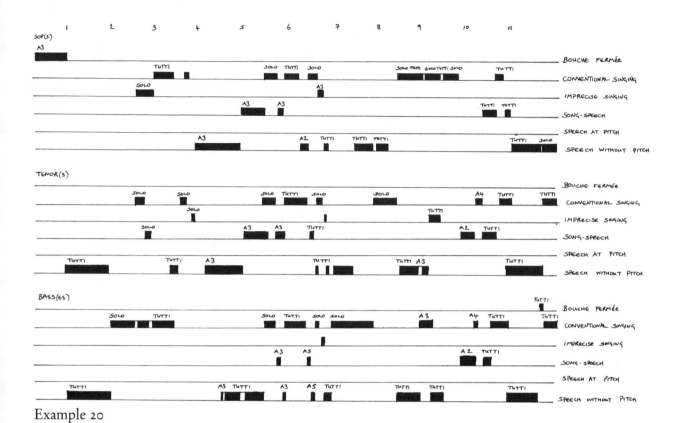

Example 20

The piece opens with the two extremes, *bouche fermée* singing and speech without pitch. Male voices are more consistently than female voices associated with speech without pitch, but, ultimately, the roles are reversed, so that the basses touch the extreme of *bouche fermée* singing and finish with conventional singing, while the solo soprano reaches speech without pitch (Example 20).

As in *Le visage nuptial*, Boulez seeks a connection between poetry and music not only on the level of 'morphological structures' but, also, on the level of 'affective relations'. Several memorable points of 'affective relations' spring to mind. The striking, *fortissimo* entry of the male voices in the very first line, which is combined with a sudden increase in tempo, serves very well as a musical equivalent for the image of the 'River setting forth too soon,

Example 21

Example 22

at one bound . . .' The echo effect achieved on the words *Rivière souvent punie, rivière à l'abandon* (River often punished, river neglected) is also noteworthy (Examples 21, 22).

In *Le visage nuptial* and *Le soleil des eaux*, Boulez's departure from conventional practice was mainly in the realm of vocal emission: his idea of poetry as an 'irrigation' of music was only beginning to develop. His observance of the poems' inner and outer structure, of the syntactic logic of the poems, and of the expressive or 'affective' relationships between the poetry and the music, were not features which were entirely new in the setting of poetry. The great length of the texts was partly responsible for restricting the exploration of new relationships between text and music. Nevertheless, in *Le visage nuptial* and *Le soleil des eaux*, Boulez formed the basis of his attitude to the problems of setting poetry to music and laid the groundwork for his important vocal works of the fifties and sixties.

René Char: Le marteau sans maître

In discussion of Boulez's *Le marteau sans maître* (1953–55),[13] which is based on three poems extracted from Char's collection of the same name, published first in 1945, it will become possible to throw greater light on Boulez's idiosyncratic ideas about poetry as the 'irrigation' of music and as a 'centre and absence'.

Le marteau sans maître is divided into nine sections, containing three separate, interwoven cycles. The following are the titles of the movements as they might appear in a conventional order:

1 *Avant L'artisanat furieux*
2 *L'artisanat furieux*
3 *Après L'artisanat furieux*
4 *Bel édifice et les pressentiments, version première*
5 *Bel édifice et les pressentiments, double*
6 *Bourreaux de solitude*
7 *Commentaire 1 de Bourreaux de solitude*
8 *Commentaire 2 de Bourreaux de solitude*
9 *Commentaire 3 de Bourreaux de solitude*

Each vocal setting has some sort of commentary on it: *L'artisanat furieux* has a prelude and postlude, which are both instrumental pieces; *Bel édifice et les pressentiments* has a *double*, which is a second vocal setting, and *Bourreaux de solitude* has three instrumental commentaries. Boulez does not observe this order, however: instead, he mixes them up so that a vocal setting will never be followed directly by one of its commentaries, nor will two commentaries on the same poem follow each other. The order of the

13. Boulez worked on *Le marteau* between 1953 and 1955. It was first performed on 18 June 1955 in Baden-Baden. The work was revised in 1957.

pieces as they appear in Boulez's score, together with the instrumentation, is as follows:

1	*Avant L'artisanat furieux*	Flute, vibraphone, guitar, viola
2	*Commentaire 1 de Bourreaux de solitude*	Flute, xylorimba, drum, 2 bongos, viola
3	*L'artisanat furieux*	Voice, flute
4	*Commentaire 2 de Bourreaux de solitude*	Xylorimba, vibraphone, small cymbals, tubular bells, triangle, guitar, viola
5	*Bel édifice et les pressentiments, version première*	Voice, flute
6	*Bourreaux de solitude*	Voice, flute, xylorimba, vibraphone, maracas, guitar, viola
7	*Après L'artisanat furieux*	Flute, vibraphone, guitar
8	*Commentaire 3 de Bourreaux de solitude*	Flute, xylorimba, vibraphone, claves, tubular bells, 2 bongos, maracas
9	*Bel édifice et les pressentiments, double*	Voice, flute, xylorimba, vibraphone, tom-tom, large gong, very large tom-tom, large suspended cymbal, guitar, viola

Boulez does not confuse the order of the movements out of mere capriciousness. The unorthodox order of movements can be explained in terms of Char's 'verbal archipelago', an idea at the very base of Char's poetic technique. The images of a poem are compared to the islands of an archipelago; it is possible to go from one island to another in any sequence and, each time, to accumulate a different set of experiences. The reader is a traveller among images; he may take any route and any conclusion is valid. The idea of the archipelago can be applied to poems, as well as to images or individual words. Boulez adopts the idea for the sequence of musical pieces. It was a dissatisfaction with conventional styles of development, the logic of two and two makes four,[14] that led to this new approach:

For the moment we only wish to suggest a musical work where this division into homogeneous movements would be abandoned in favour of a non-homogeneous distribution of developments. Let us reclaim for music the right to parentheses and italics...an idea of discontinuous time thanks to structures which are interwoven instead of remaining partitioned and watertight, in fact a sort of development where the closed circuit is not the only foreseeable solution.[15]

Boulez's adoption of the archipelago technique is a prime exam-

14. See the extract from Artaud's 'Lettre aux recteurs des universités européennes', in Chapter II.
15. Pierre Boulez, 'Recherches maintenant', *R.A.*, p 32.

ple of poetry as an 'irrigation' of music, not restricted to affective relationships but defining the underlying structure. The idea of poetry as 'centre and absence' of the music is also at work in *Le marteau*. The poem is the 'centre' because it defines so many features of the music and 'absent' because, in many places, the poetry is not actually heard. For example, the poem *Bourreaux de solitude* is at the centre of *Commentaire 1 de Bourreaux de solitude* but the poem is not actually sung. The idea of 'centre and absence' can also be applied to the vocal settings:

Contrary to this commonly held opinion, it seems that one can act on the intelligibility of a text as 'centre or absence' of the music. If you wish to 'understand' the text, then read it! or have it spoken to you; there will be no better solution. The more subtle work that I propose to you now assumes that a knowledge of the poem has already been acquired.[16]

Here, Boulez is suggesting that the listener should be familiar with the text that the composer sets and let his knowledge of the poem colour his appreciation of the music. In this case, the text is the 'centre' of the appreciation, as it colours the listener's reception of the music, but 'absent' in that the listener need not listen to the text itself. The idea of 'centre and absence' is obviously important in *Le marteau* in the instrumental commentaries on the music. Here the concepts of 'centre and absence' and the archipelago are closely bound up, the two ideas being interdependent.

The three texts from Char's collection follow in the order in which they appear as vocal settings:

1 *L'artisanat furieux*
La roulotte rouge au bord du clou
Et cadavre dans le panier
Et chevaux de labours dans le fer à cheval
Je rêve la tête sur la pointe de mon couteau le Pérou.

Furious artisans
The red caravan at the edge of the prison
And corpse in the basket
And workhorses in the horse shoe
I dream my head on the point of my knife, Peru.

2 *Bel édifice et les pressentiments*
J'écoute marcher dans mes jambes
La mer morte vagues par-dessus tête

Enfant la jetée-promenade sauvage
Homme l'illusion imitée

Des yeux purs dans les bois
Cherchent en pleurant la tête habitable.

Beautiful building and premonitions
I hear walking in my legs
The dead sea waves over my head

Child the wild jetty-promenade
Man the imitated illusion

Pure eyes in the woods
Weeping seek the head to live in.

3 *Bourreaux de solitude*
Le pas s'est éloigné le marcheur s'est tu
Sur le cadran de l'Imitation
Le Balancier lance sa charge de granit réflexe.

Hangmen of solitude
The footstep has receded the walker is silent
On the dial of Imitation
The Pendulum sets in motion its load of reflex granite.

16. Pierre Boulez, 'Son et verbe', *R.A.*, p 60.

Following the archipelago technique of accumulation of images, it is possible to read the text as a commentary on the hopelessness of political involvement, the inevitable failure of revolution and political idealism. The opening line of the first poem, significantly entitled *L'artisanat furieux*, presents one aspect of an unacceptable society – the repressive institution of the prison. The image of the corpse in the basket reinforces the morbid implications. The last line describes the extreme tension of the narrator. Its image is very powerful, containing an immediate threat of violence. The dream it mentions may represent the dream of revolution and the realisation of political ideals which will lead to the narrator's death should he awake and try to realise them.

The title of the second poem brings us to another side of an unequal society. If *bel édifice* represents the wealthy in society, then *les pressentiments* may refer to imminent political upheaval. The movement implied in the first line may be the movement of revolution, and *la mer morte*, from the second, may represent the decaying society. Perhaps youth, compared to a wild promenade pier, can achieve the change, but the *enfant* of the third line soon becomes the *homme* of the fourth and he is *l'illusion imitée*, hollow and vain. The *yeux purs* of idealism can find no home, despite their *cherchent en pleurant*.

The failure of idealism which becomes apparent from the line *homme l'illusion imitée* is reinforced in the last stanza. The *pas* of the revolution has receded and the idealist is silent. The last image of the poem is a very potent one. The pendulum with its load of granite may represent the intractable and unalterable swing of society. Although a pendulum moves, it does not go anywhere – it just drives the cogs relentlessly.

Perhaps this reading is too simple and too obvious. No doubt there are many possible interpretations, but it is probable that almost any account will bring out the inherent pessimism of the poems. Whatever the interpretation, the transition from movement to stillness cannot be denied.

In comparing these poems to the five poems of *Le visage nuptial*, one point of difference stands out – the great disparity in length between the groups. Boulez has given the following explanation of his turn to shorter verse:

Since my ideas about setting a poem to music have little in common with the usual conceptions, I found that Char's condensation of the word was a great help. . .If a text is too extended the time becomes so expanded that music can no longer have any *raison d'être* in relation to it. In Char's poetry on the other hand, where time is extremely concentrated, music does not distend time but can be grafted on to it. Such a poem does not defy music but invites it. So this is another way in which Char's poetry attracted me. In the three works *Le visage nuptial*, *Le soleil des eaux* and *Le marteau sans maître*, I was progressively reducing things: in other words, in *Le visage nuptial* the text is long whereas in *Le marteau sans maître* I chose the shortest poems, of just a few lines, which allowed me to have a completely different conception of the relation between poetry and music – no longer as a simple meeting between poetry and music, but as a graft in which music and poem can retain their independence up to a point.[17]

The concentration of time that Boulez speaks of is clearly visible in the three poems from *Le marteau*, where a large span of movement is described in very few words. This gives Boulez the freedom to extend the setting, to comment on it instrumentally from several different angles and to explore the implications of the text in music. Short provocative texts of this nature allow Boulez to achieve the ideals of relationship between sound and word that were mentioned in discussion of *Le visage nuptial*. The 'tissue of conjunctions' between poetry and music that Boulez seeks is much stronger and more subtle in *Le marteau* than in his earlier vocal works.

In *Le visage nuptial*, the text defined the form of the music in the most obvious way. The text was so long that there was little room for instrumental commentary, and the composer's choice in the matter of form was severely limited. In *Le marteau*, however, the brief texts present the composer with more flexible material and allow him much more scope in the choice of form. In the vocal settings Boulez places the vocal lines in alternation with instrumental passages in such a way that a symmetrical pattern is formed. The symmetry that Boulez imposes on the music is a realisation in musical terms of the symmetries inherent in the poetry. *Bel édifice et les pressentiments*, for example, divides into three groups of two lines. In reading the poem, one would pause naturally after each couplet. One might, also, make a short pause between the lines of the second couplet in order to emphasise the contrast of the images. Char's severely condensed verse requires a carefully balanced reading. Having observed Boulez's sensitive treatment of Char's verse in *Le visage nuptial*, one experiences no surprise in finding that he observes this balanced 'reading' in his setting. In *Bel édifice et les pressentiments, double* we hear the first couplet followed by a long instrumental interlude; the first line of the second couplet followed by a shorter instrumental interlude; then the second line of the second couplet. The last couplet is separated from the second couplet by an instrumental interlude and a pause. Expressed diagrammatically, the following symmetrical pattern emerges:

17. *C.D.*, p 44.

———————————

———————————

inst. interlude

———————————

inst. interlude

———————————

inst. interlude (pause)

———————————

———————————

The shape is a highly satisfactory one, reminiscent, perhaps, of Bartók's arch forms. Moreover, it expresses in musical terms the shape of the poetry. Whilst doing as little damage as possible to the original poetic conception, Boulez achieves the amalgam between poetry and music that he speaks of in 'Son et verbe'. A similar approach governs the other vocal movements.

Although the shorter texts allow Boulez more freedom in respect of form, his feeling for the French language prevents him from abusing it. As Stockhausen points out: 'The vocal composition always clarifies the phonological structure of the French text in syllable, word and phrase. . .'[18] In the first line of *Bel édifice et les pressentiments*, *double*, for example, the division of the phrases is quite natural, remembering that Char's condensed verse requires a balanced and unhurried delivery: 'J'écoute marcher   dans mes jambes   la mer morte   vagues par-dessus tête'.

Boulez's sensitive handling of individual words of the French language can be seen in his setting of words like *morte* and *homme*. In normal diction, the final 'e' of such words is spoken very softly, being more the result of the momentum of the preceding syllable than of a deliberate pronunciational effort. In *Bel édifice et les pressentiments, version première*, Boulez sets the final 'e' of *morte* and *homme* with a grace note, thus allowing the singer the freedom to pronounce the word as naturally as possible (Example 23). The same technique is applied to the words *promenade* and *sauvage* in the same piece (Example 24a). Where Boulez does not provide a grace note for such weak syllables, he lets the syllable fall as naturally as possible on a weak division of the beat (Example 24b).

In *Le marteau*, Boulez adopts a much more sober approach to the question of vocal emission. Two of the four vocal movements are sung in the normal way. These are *L'artisanat furieux* and *Bour-*

18. Karlheinz Stockhausen, 'Music and Speech', *Die Reihe*, vi (1964), p 44.

LA - MER —— MORTE

HOMME

Example 23

LA JE - TÉE - PRO - ME - NA —— DE

Example 24b

TÊ - TE

SAU —— VAGE

Example 24a

reaux de solitude. Bel édifice et les pressentiments, version première and *Bel édifice et les pressentiments, double* make restricted use of vocal effects. The employment of these effects can be most clearly observed in *Bel édifice et les pressentiments, double*, the final movement of *Le marteau*. Boulez is less precise about the effects he requires in *Le marteau* than in *Le visage nuptial*: there is no table of 'conventions' and there are only three unusual symbols used. The first of these is like Schoenberg's *Sprechgesang* symbol and Boulez's 'song–speech' symbol of *Le visage nuptial*. It consists of a normal note with a cross marked on its stem. This notation appears in *Bel édifice et les pressentiments, double* with the instruction *quasi parlando* marked above it. A certain amount of ambiguity enters here. Boulez appears to ask the singer to sing 'as if speaking'. The effect he requires is probably closer to Schoenberg's *Sprechgesang* than the 'song–speech' of *Le visage nuptial*, which asks the singer to start each note on an exact pitch and then to change to speech style. The second unusual symbol is like the symbol for 'speech at pitch' of *Le visage nuptial*. It is only employed on monotones and seems to fulfil the same function. The third new symbol involves the use of diamond note heads. This symbol is not explained when it appears first in *Bel édifice et les pressentiments, version première*, but is marked *détimbrer* when it appears in *Bel édifice et les pressentiments, double*. One assumes that it always implies a reduction of tone quality wherever it appears. There are also one or two verbal instructions. Apart from the instructions *quasi parlando* and *détimbrer*, the words *quasi crié* (as if shouted) and *voix de tête* (head tone) also appear. In addition to those variations of normal tone production, Boulez once more asks for *bouche fermée* singing.

The relatively restricted range of vocal techniques, and the imprecise instructions governing their use in *Le marteau*, contrast with their extensive use and copious instructions in *Le visage nuptial*. There is a noticeable shift of emphasis from a preoccupation with gradations of vocal emission to a concern with form and structure. This shift of emphasis is partly explained, of course, by the nature of the texts, a shorter text offering less opportunity for the exploration of new techniques. It is also possible that Boulez came to a realisation that the seven vocal techniques of *Le visage nuptial* were too similar to each other, the subtlety of the gradation of tone being lost on the audience, even if the singer was able to reproduce them consistently.

In *Bel édifice et les pressentiments, double* there are four styles of vocal production:

1 speech at pitch (on monotones only)
2 *quasi parlando*
3 normal singing
4 *bouche fermée* singing

In his article 'Music and Speech', Stockhausen identifies a further category between the extremes of pure music (*bouche fermée* singing) and speech. He divides the category of normal singing into syllabic song and melismatic song. Stockhausen quite rightly argues that 'musical parameters are dominant' in the category of melismatic song, giving us 'more tones than syllables'.[19] In *Bel édifice et les pressentiments, double* the voice passes from one extreme to another in terms of vocal production. The first two lines are sung *quasi parlando*: the third and fourth are 'spoken at pitch'; the fifth and sixth lines are sung syllabically and melismatically; and *bouche fermée* singing separates the couplets. In the closing stages of the

19. Ibid, p 47.

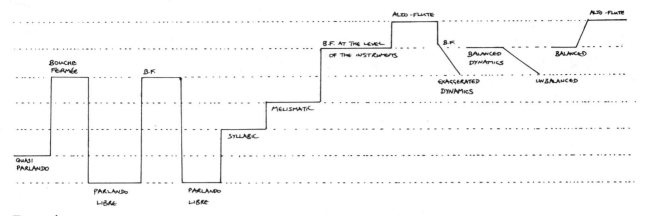

Example 25

movement, the voice is instructed to sing *au niveau des instruments, bouche fermée, pas en soloiste* (at the [dynamic] level of the instruments, mouth closed, not as a soloist). Here the transition from speech to pure music is complete, as the voice is absorbed into the overall tone colour of the ensemble. Stockhausen has provided an excellent diagram showing the transition from speech to pure music and, as it shows, the voice varies in dynamics towards the end, sometimes rising above the level of the instruments but finally returning to the level of the ensemble (Example 25). This is another and more sophisticated instance of techniques of vocal production defining the form of a piece. It also illustrates the integration of music and poetry on the formal level.

Despite the limitation of vocal effects that Boulez imposes on the other three vocal movements, he does not ignore the 'affective' or expressive relationship between music and poetry. The flurry of notes on the word *cadavre* in *L'artisanat furieux* surely has an expressive function (Example 26). Notice also the expressive role of the instruments in *Bel édifice et les pressentiments, version première*, where the word *marcher* from the phrase *j'écoute marcher* is accompanied by homorhythmic chords (Example 27). The infrequent occurrence of rhythmic unisons of this sort makes the example more striking. Further 'affective' relationships between voice and instruments will be pointed out in the analysis of *Bourreaux de solitude* which follows.

Bourreaux de solitude: the problem of analysis

Le marteau is in many ways a pinnacle in the career of Pierre Boulez. With *Le marteau*, Boulez gained international renown, performances of it being given in major European capitals, and, in

Example 26

1957, it won the prize of the Académie Charles Gros. *Le marteau* asserted Boulez's leadership of the avant-garde, its technique of total serialism was widely adopted and its 'gamelan' ensemble had a lasting influence on còmposers. In *Le marteau*, several of Boulez's theories about the relation of music to poetry, and about the composition of music in general, came to fruition. In short, *Le marteau* represents the culmination of a period of research and experimentation. It seems appropriate, therefore, to take a detailed look at one of the movements from *Le marteau*. Not only will this take us more deeply into Boulez's early masterpiece but it will amplify some of the points made in foregoing chapters.

Although *Le marteau* is a product of total serialism, the technique is not applied in a totalitarian way. Boulez's experience with *Polyphonie X* of 1951 had taught him the dangers of the rigid application of total serialism. *Polyphonie X*, Boulez feels, suffers from 'theoretical exaggeration'.[20] (The 'X' in the title is not a Roman numeral but a graphic symbol describing the intersection of series.) Despite its disastrous first performance, *Polyphonie X* was often heard in Darmstadt alongside Stockhausen's *Kontra-Punkte* and seems to have exerted a considerable influence on composers. Boulez, however, was not happy with it. In an article of 1954, he attacked composers who applied serial techniques too rigidly:

Not everything is for the best in the realm of the series. . .One comes to certain conclusions, showing zeal in exploiting, amplifying them; one throws oneself frenziedly on organisation; feeling oneself to be on the edge of unexploited worlds – The Promised Land or Babel would hardly be misplaced comparisons. Webern only organised pitch, we organise rhythm, timbre, dynamics; all is fodder for this monstrous polyvalent organisation which must be hushed if we are not going to be condemned to deafness. We will soon see that composition and organisation cannot be confused – something which Webern himself never thought of doing – on pain of maniacal inanity.[21]

Boulez's warning against the mechanical application of a system is reminiscent of warnings issued by Schoenberg about the series, and by Le Corbusier about the Modular:

20. *C.D.*, p 58.
21. Pierre Boulez, 'Recherches maintenant', *R.A.*, pp 28–29.

Example 27

Do you imagine that the 'Modular' is a panacea for clumsiness and carelessness?
. . .If all you can do is produce such horrors as these, drop it. Your eyes are your
judges, the only ones you should know. . .The 'Modular' is a working tool, a
precision instrument; a keyboard shall we say, a piano, a *tuned* piano. The piano
has been tuned: it is up to you to play it well. The 'Modular' does not confer talent,
still less genius. It does not make the dull subtle: it only offers them the facility of a
sure measure. But out of the unlimited choice of the 'Modular' the choice is
yours.[22]

Schoenberg also stresses the importance of the artistic contribution.
The system is a means to an end, not an end in itself:

The introduction of my method of composing with twelve notes does not
facilitate composing; on the contrary, it makes it more difficult. The restrictions
imposed on the composer by the obligation to use only one set are so severe that
they can only be overcome by an imagination which has survived a tremendous
number of adventures. . .One has to follow the basic set but nevertheless one
composes as freely as before.[23]

Having established a new technique of composition with *Structures*, and having created a new vocabulary and syntax, Boulez set
about refining his technique. Flexibility, a feature that Boulez feels
is essential to musical invention, had to be reintroduced, and this is
what he did in *Le marteau*:

[*Le marteau*] takes account of affective phenomena associated with music. For
this reason the technique had to be infinitely more supple and lend itself to all
kinds of invention. . .There is in fact a very clear element of control, but starting
from this strict control and the work's overall discipline there is also room for
what I call *local indiscipline*: at the overall level there is discipline and control, at
the local level there is an element of indiscipline – a freedom to choose, to decide
and to reject.[24]

Ironically, it is this very element of freedom and 'local indiscipline' in the context of a strict control which makes analysis of *Le
marteau* so very difficult, as Boulez himself says: 'a technical
analysis of *Le marteau sans maître* would certainly be much more
difficult than one of *Polyphonie*.' The problem, then, is to differentiate the elements which are derived from the strict overall control
from the elements which are the result of local indiscipline. The
problem is compounded by the complexity of Boulez's technique.
Unfortunately, Boulez's account of his technique, the Darmstadt
lectures published as *On music today*, is of little help.

Here, Boulez describes his technique largely by analogy with
arithmetical procedures. Moreover, his application of scientific or
arithmetical terms is often approximate. Take, for example, his use
of the words 'density' and 'weight' in the third of the following four
categories in a 'network of possibilities' for each component (pitch,
duration, timbre, etc.):

22. Le Corbusier, *The modular*
London, 1954, p 109.
23. Arnold Schoenberg, *Style and idea*
London, 1951, p 114, pp 116–17.
24. *C.D.*, p 66.

1 *Absolute value* within a defining interval, or module; each value will occur only once, within this module, a value being defined in relation to some unit of division of the space in question;

2 *Relative value*, that is to say, value considered as the absolute value reproduced by addition to multiples of the module, from 1 to n times: each absolute value will have from 1 to n corresponding relative values;

3 *Fixed density of generation*: each original X will correspond to a Y of the same type and weight, the index of density being established as a fixed value between 1 and n;

4 *Mobile density of generation*: each X will correspond, by transformation, to a Y of different type and weight.[25]

Properly used, the word 'density' refers to a relation of mass and volume, while 'weight' refers to a relation of mass and gravity. By talking about weight instead of density, Boulez introduces the new aspect of gravity. It would, perhaps, have been more accurate to use the word 'mass' instead of 'weight' but even then Boulez's exact meaning is not clear.

By talking of a 'fixed density of generation' and referring to a relationship of X and Y, Boulez seems to be describing a graph in which the relation between the components is constant – in other words a straight-line graph (Example 28). This arithmetical idea is used analogously to describe a relationship between notes. In the graph, each figure of the X axis relates to a figure of the Y axis. When $X = Y - 2$, the figures of the Y axis will always be larger than the figures of the X axis to which they are related. In musical terms, if one takes a series of notes, expressed by their semitonal relationship to the starting point, and calls these figures the X axis, then, following the same formula, each X will correlate with a Y that is larger by 2:

0, 2, 11, 8, 10 becomes
2, 4, 1, 10, 0;
(where numbers add up to 12 or more, 12 is subtracted).

Believe it or not, this constitutes a simple upward transposition by one tone (Example 29)! Why does Boulez feel it necessary to describe simple musical phenomena by such roundabout means? There are two answers. First, the function of the graph when applied to pitch relationships in this way may seem obvious, but the graph can be used to relate different components (pitch, duration, dynamics, timbre). Moreover, the fourth category in the 'network of possibilities' seems to describe relationships of notes other than through 'fixed density' – the straight-line graph. 'Mobile density' may imply a relationship of X and Y through a parabolic curve, for example. In short, the system only seems to overcomplicate the issue when it is applied to simple musical phenomena – its value becomes apparent in more complex procedures. Second, this

25. *O.M.T.*, p 38.

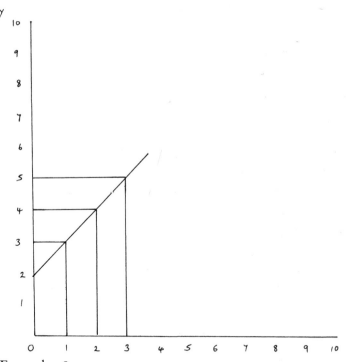

Example 28: x = y − 2

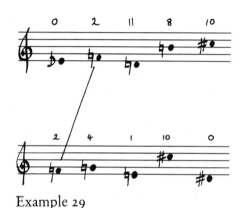

Example 29

exposition is intended to describe Boulez's technique as he conceived it. Just as he arrives at musical form by analogy with poetry, so he arrives at his musical technique by analogy with mathematics. To simplify his procedure would have been to falsify the issue. We can only regret, with the confused Mr Northcott, that this book is so difficult and that so 'many terms appear without detailed explanation' and that 'the relation of the text to musical examples is, in places, elliptical to say the least'.[26]

An analysis of *Le marteau* is, therefore, an ambitious project. One can hardly expect to explain every note: some points, however, can be made with some degree of certainty. In the following consideration of *Bourreaux de solitude*, attention is focused first on pitch and duration. This approach was prompted by Boulez's comment that 'pitch and duration seem to form the basis of a compositional dialectic'.[27] A simple relationship of rhythmic values and pitches was discovered. Before the entry of the voice in bar 13, the music can be divided into six sections, each of which presents the twelve semitones in twelve different note values. In the first section, the note D is one semiquaver in length, D sharp is two, E is three and so on until one reaches C sharp, which is twelve semiquavers in length. The relationship of pitches to duration values can be expressed by one of Boulez's straight-line graphs of

26. Bayan Northcott, 'Boulez's theory of composition', *Music and Musicians*, xx (1971), p 32.
27. *O.M.T.*, p 37.

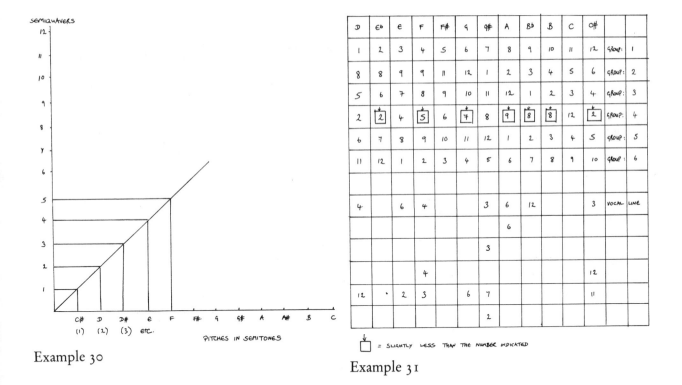

Example 30

Example 31

↓ □ = SLIGHTLY LESS THAN THE NUMBER INDICATED

'fixed density of generation' (Example 30). In each of the six sections, the same principle applies. In the second section, the shortest note value is G sharp which is one semiquaver, then A which is two, and so on. There is 'indiscipline' in this group where D and E flat are both eight semiquavers in length and E and F are both nine semiquavers long. In the third group, B flat is the shortest note. In the fourth group, the introduction of triplet rhythms leads to some approximation of semiquaver values. In the fifth group, the system becomes perfectly regular again, the shortest note being A. The system remains regular in the sixth group, where the shortest note is E. In Example 31, the notes and their note values have been plotted, and the working of the system can be clearly seen here. The approach to duration and its relationship to pitch is reminiscent of Messiaen's approach in *Mode de valeurs et d'intensités*. The difference between Messiaen's and Boulez's techniques is the difference between modal and serial composition. In Messiaen's system, each note had a fixed value which remained the same throughout the composition (Example 7). In Boulez's system, however, each note can have one of twelve values, providing it falls in the series of pitch and duration.

Although the length of the notes is determined by serial procedure, the placing of the notes is governed by aesthetic considerations. In the opening thirteen bars, the notes are placed in such a

Example 32

Example 33

D	Eb	E	F	F#	G	G#	A	Bb	B	C	C#		
$\overset{>}{MF}$	MF	$\overset{>}{MP}$	MP	$\overline{P}$	P	$\overline{PP}$	PP	FF/SFZ	FF	F/SFZ	F	GROUP:	1
$\overline{PP}$	PP	FF/SFZ	FF	F/SFZ	F	$\overset{>}{MF}$	MF	MP	MP	$\overline{P}$	P	GROUP:	2
FF/SFZ	FF	FF/SFZ	F	$\overset{>}{MF}$	MF	$\overset{>}{MP}$	MP	P	PP	$\overline{PP}$	PP	GROUP:	3
F	$\overset{>}{MF}$	MF	$\overset{>}{MP}$	MP	$\overline{P}$	P	$\overline{PP}$	PP	FF/SFZ	FF	F/SFZ	GROUP:	4
PP	FF/SFZ	FF		$\overset{>}{MF}$	MF		MP	$\overline{P}$		PP		GROUP:	5
F	F	$\overline{P}$	P	$\overline{PP}$	PP	FF/SFZ	FF	FF/SFZ	F	$\overset{>}{MP}$	MF	GROUP:	6
FF		F	$\overset{>}{MF}$			MP	$\overline{PP}$	P			VOCAL	LINE	
		$\overset{>}{MF}$					FF/SFZ						
					FF/SFZ								

Example 34

way as to create an overall regular rhythm. In Example 32, the entries of the notes have been plotted. Bar 1 consists of three groups of semiquavers, bar 2 contains entries spaced at a quaver distance. The pause of bar 5 is followed by two bars of triplets. It seems appropriate that poems with important images of walking and movement should be set with such regular rhythms. It is significant that the rhythm becomes disrupted at the words *le marcheur s'est tu*. It becomes sporadic, suggesting a change from organised movement to random purposeless activity (Example 33).

While Boulez describes pitch and duration as the 'basis of a compositional dialectic', intensity and timbre belong to 'secondary categories'.[28] In the opening thirteen bars, dynamics are applied in the same way as pitch and rhythm. (Twelve dynamics are employed: *pp*; *pp* with *tenuto*; *p*; *p* with *tenuto*; *mp*; *mp* with *accent*; *mf*; *mf* with *accent*; *f*; *f* marked *sforzando*; *ff*; *ff* marked *sforzando*.) There is one difference in application, however. Whereas the rhythms become larger as the pitches rise, the dynamics reduce or become softer as the pitches rise (Example 34). The application of the dynamics in the opening bars is carried out with very few deviations from the system.

The serialisation of dynamics raises a problem of practicality. Is it possible for six players to maintain a differentiation of the twelve dynamics with any accuracy and consistency? The problem becomes more acute when one player has two or more notes in different dynamics (see, for example, the xylorimba part in bar 6). It seems that a certain amount of approximation is inevitable. Perhaps the use of twelve different dynamics is, therefore, something of a 'theoretical exaggeration'. The use of continually varied dynamics, however, will encourage a pointillist style of performance. Some of Boulez's dynamic instructions are simply impossible, however. See, for example, the *crescendo* in the guitar part in bar 1 and the *crescendo* in the vibraphone part in bar 4.

While the first thirteen bars contain a presentation of the twelve notes of the semitonal scale in varied dynamics and durations according to serial technique, after the voice entry in bar 13 a certain degree of selectivity is introduced and the simple pitch–rhythm and pitch–dynamic relationships of the opening appear to break down. The entry of the voice part is prepared by a thinning of the texture and, in this respect, Boulez's setting is quite traditional. The voice enters in unison with the alto flute and this immediately establishes a different relationship among the instruments. Instruments adopt a supportive role to the voice, which implies some duplication of pitch and preference of pitch areas. As the first vocal phrase enters in unison with the alto flute, so it ends in unison with the viola (bar 17). A precedent for the duplication of pitches has now been set.

28. *O.M.T.*, p 37.

The notes D and A of the alto flute in bars 17 to 19 are taken up by guitar in bars 18 and 19. The viola also introduces an A in bar 17. The compositional approach has undergone a drastic change. No longer are we presented with groups of semitonal saturations; instead, 'pockets' of pitch areas are presented. In bars 17 and 18, the notes D and A are important. In bars 24 and 25, the notes E flat and C assume importance. In bars 24 and 25, the voice phrase *s'est tu* on the notes E flat and C is taken up by guitar and viola. Notice also the guitar C which precedes the phrase and the flute C which follows it. A system of greater or lesser selectivity governs the body of the piece until bar 79, *ancora meno lento*, where semitonal saturations are again heard, although a certain degree of pitch preference is retained within the context of the saturation. Notice, for example, the recurrence of the notes E and F in bars 86 and 87 and the notes B and B flat in bar 91.

In *Bourreaux de solitude*, form is defined not by contrast of key or theme, but by contrast of pitch saturation and selection. The selection of pitch areas in the centre of the movement contrasts with the semitonal saturations of the beginning and closing stages of the movement. The three sections could be described in the following terms. Bars 1 to 13 act as an exposition, presenting six semitonal saturations in which each note has a different duration. The procedure provides a continually altering hierarchy of the notes – the longest being the most important. Each time the hierarchy changes, a different perspective of the saturation is provided.

The central section acts as a development. The focus continues to change as different notes assume importance. There is still a changing hierarchy, but it is applied in a different way. The selectivity also allows contrast of texture and a certain amount of 'affective' relationship between voice and instruments.

The final section creates a synthesis of the exposition and development sections, retaining the selectivity of pitches within the context of semitonal saturation. The form is a ternary one, defined not by theme but by technique. It can be compared to classical sonata form, where two contrasted ideas are presented and a synthesis is finally formed from them. This is not to say that *Bourreaux de solitude* is in sonata form, merely that the underlying process is similar.

While it has been possible to explain the function of the areas of pitch preference, the method that Boulez uses to select these pitches is not so easy to discover. The pitch–rhythm chart (Example 31) illustrates the preference of pitches and the abandonment of the arithmetical progression of the opening. While bars 1 to 13 probably come under the first category of Boulez's 'network of possibilities', which describes an arithmetical progression, the areas of pitch selection may fall under the category of 'relative value', which could be interpreted as describing a relationship of notes in geometrical progression. It is possible to identify places where Boulez may be applying a system of geometrical progression in *Bourreaux de solitude*. For example, the numbers in the first vocal line, 3, 6, 12, are related to each other in geometrical progression (Example 31). How, then, does one explain the notes C sharp, D, E and F which do not fall into the progression? Perhaps they can be explained in terms of 'local indiscipline'. It could be that Boulez allows himself freedom in treating the vocal part. It could also be that there is another system operating here. It is at this point that the element of 'local indiscipline' hinders analysis, for the failings of any proposed systems can be explained away in these terms.

Looking at Example 31, we see that, although all twelve semitones are not being presented, some of the notes can be arranged into arithmetical progression. If the system of a direct relationship of pitches to durations in arithmetical progression is still in operation, how then can one explain the selection of pitches? Looking at the second to bottom line of the diagram, we see that the numbers 3, 6, and 12, occur. But, if this is a geometrical progression, how then does one explain the numbers 2, 7, 11, that occur alongside them? Unfortunately, these questions remain unanswered. For present purposes, it suffices to say that a system of selection of pitches is in operation. The system is applied with a greater or lesser degree of strictness and its function is both formal and colouristic. One can only hope that the threads of the research that are left here will be taken up again. It will, no doubt, take several minds to untangle the process of Boulez's musical thought in this work, which is so subtle a blend of discipline and freedom.

IV · Poetic Confrontation II:
A Throw of the Dice

What we must do from now on, following the examples
of Joyce and Mallarmé, is to stop regarding the work as a
simple trajectory, traced between point of departure and
point of arrival.

Boulez, 1963[1]

Mountain ranges often form boundaries between one region and
another or between one nation and another. As we have seen, *Le
marteau* formed a pinnacle in Boulez's career: it was the result of
researches into compositional technique and various relations of
poetry and music, and it also marked the high point of his leadership
of the avant-garde. Like a mountain range, *Le marteau* may also be
seen as a dividing line in Boulez's career. On one side of the line falls
Boulez's preoccupation with the condensed, violent poetry of his
contemporary, René Char. On the other side falls his interest in the
innovative, enigmatic poetry of the nineteenth-century symbolist,
Stéphane Mallarmé. Before *Le marteau*, Boulez was an uncompromising front-runner in the avant-garde. After *Le marteau*, he
seems more often to be following trends than creating them. In the
early years, Boulez's style was rigorous and sometimes even
abrasive. In later years, his technique allowed more freedom and
much of his music appears more improvisatory in character and
more relaxed in mood.

Although changes in Boulez's style before and after *Le marteau*
can be observed, a considerable element of continuity remains.
Boulez may have crossed a mountain range and entered another
region, but his language remains the same – only his dialect alters.
Perhaps the climate changes a little, too. This new region is, by
contrast, a temperate zone.

One feature that Boulez carried through from the period up to
and including *Le marteau* is his preoccupation with the formal
implications of poetry for music. The short texts of *Le marteau*
allowed Boulez to create a more effective graft of poetry and music,
and it is not surprising to find that the Mallarmé texts which Boulez

1. Pierre Boulez, 'Sonate, que me veux-
tu?', *Perspectives of New Music*, i, 2
(1963), p 32.

chose to set were also short, provocative ones in symmetrical forms. Before setting Mallarmé's sonnets, however, Boulez set a protracted text by Henri Michaux.

Henri Michaux: *Poésie pour pouvoir*

In this work Boulez set two poems from a group under the collective title of *Poésie pour pouvoir* (Poetry for power). The title of the collection reflects one of Michaux's main preoccupations, the power of poetry to assert the poet's authority. It also hints at the poet's fascination with magical ritual and incantation. Michaux's ideas are rather unusual and perhaps require a word of explanation. Michaux is not so much concerned with the expression of emotion as with the creation of an experience, the prime importance of which is for the creator, helping him to realise his full efficacy as an individual. In this respect, the writing of the poem is more important than the poem itself. Poetry, Michaux feels, can act as a healing response to the destructiveness of experience. Just as experience invades the poet, so will the poet invade other experiences. In *Je rame* and *À travers mers et désert*, there is no element of defensiveness. More than eighty lines are devoted to an attack on an unnamed person in a malevolent incantation.

<table>
<tr><td>

Je rame

J'ai maudit ton front ton ventre ta vie
J'ai maudit les rues que ta marche enfile
Les objets que ta main saisit
J'ai maudit l'intérieur de tes rêves

J'ai mis une flaque dans ton œil qui ne voit plus
Un insecte dans ton oreille qui n'entend plus
Une éponge dans ton cerveau qui ne comprend plus

Je t'ai refroidi en l'âme de ton corps
Je t'ai glacé en ta vie profonde
L'air que tu respires te suffoque
L'air que tu respires a un air de cave
Est un air qui a déjà été expiré
   qui a été rejeté par des hyènes
Le fumier de cet air personne ne peut plus le respirer

Ta peau est toute humide
Ta peau sue l'eau de la grande peur
Tes aisselles dégagent au loin une odeur de crypte

Les animaux s'arrêtent sur ton passage
Les chiens, la nuit, hurlent, la tête levée
   vers ta maison

</td><td>

I row

I have cursed your brow your belly your life
I have cursed the roads that you walk
The objects that your hands grasp
I have cursed the interior of your dreams

I have put a puddle in your eye which no longer sees
An insect in your ear which no longer hears
A sponge in your brain which no longer understands

I have chilled you in the soul of your body
I have frozen you in the depths of your life
The air you breathe stifles you
The air you breathe is an air of cellars
Is an air already breathed out
   and rejected by hyenas

Your skin is dank
Your skin sweats in terror
Your armpits project a smell of crypts

Animals stop as you pass
Dogs howl in the night, their heads raised to your
   house

</td></tr>
</table>

Tu ne peux pas fuir
Il ne te vient pas une force de fourmi au
    bout du pied
Ta fatigue fait une souche de plomb en ton corps
Ta fatigue est une longue caravane
Ta fatigue va jusqu'au pays de Nan
Ta fatigue est inexprimable

Ta bouche te mord
Tes ongles te griffent
N'est plus à toi ta femme
N'est plus à toi ton frère
La plante de son pied est mordue par un serpent furieux

On a bavé sur ta progéniture
On a bavé sur le rire de ta fillette
On est passé en bavant devant le visage de ta demeure

Le monde s'éloigne de toi

Je rame
Je rame
Je rame contre ta vie
Je rame
Je me multiplie en rameurs innombrables
Pour ramer plus fortement contre toi

Tu tombes dans le vague
Tu es sans souffle
Tu te lasses avant même le moindre effort

Je rame
Je rame
Je rame
Tu t'en vas, ivre, attaché à la queue d'un mulet
L'ivresse comme un immense parasol qui obscurcit le
    ciel
Et assemble les mouches
L'ivresse vertigineuse des canaux semi-circulaires
Commencement mal écouté de l'hémiplégie

L'ivresse ne te quitte plus
Te couche à gauche
Te couche à droite
Te couche sur le sol pierreux du chemin
Je rame
Je rame
Je rame contre tes jours

Dans la maison de la souffrance tu entres

Je rame
Je rame
Sur un bandeau noir tes actions s'inscrivent
Sur le grand œil blanc d'un cheval borgne roule ton
    avenir

You cannot flee
Not even the power of an ant comes to the tip of your
    feet
Your weariness is a block of lead in your body
Your weariness is a long caravan
Your weariness reaches to the country of Nan
Your weariness is beyond words

Your mouth bites you
Your nails scratch you
Your wife is no longer yours
Your brother is no longer yours
The sole of his foot is bitten by a furious serpent

They have slavered on your offspring
They have slavered on your little daughter's laughter
They have slavered past the face of your home

The world withdraws from you

I row
I row
I row against your life
I row
I become innumerable rowers
To row harder against you

You fall into vagueness
You are breathless
You tire even before making the least effort

I row
I row
I row
You leave, drunk, tied to a mule's tail
Drunkenness like a great umbrella which blots out the
    sky
And attracts flies
The dizzy drunkenness of semi-circular canals
The ignored beginnings of paralysis

Drunkenness never leaves you
Fells you to the left
Fells you to the right
Fells you on the stony ground of the road
I row
I row
I row against your days

You enter the house of suffering

I row
I row
Your action is recorded on a black band
Your future rolls over the white eye of a one-eyed
    horse

À travers mers et désert

Efficace comme le coït avec une jeune fille vierge
Efficace
Efficace comme l'absence de puits dans le désert
Efficace est mon action
Efficace

Efficace comme le traître qui se tient à l'écart entouré
  de ses hommes prêts à tuer
Efficace comme la nuit pour cacher les objets
Efficace comme la chèvre pour produire des chevreaux
Petits, petits, tout navrés déjà

Efficace comme la vipère
Efficace comme le couteau effilé pour faire la plaie
Comme la rouille et l'urine pour l'entretenir
Comme les chocs, les chutes et les secousses pour
  l'agrandir
Efficace est mon action

Efficace comme le sourire de mépris pour soulever dans
  la poitrine du méprisé un océan de haine, qui jamais
  ne sera asséché
Efficace comme le désert pour déshydrater les corps et
  affermir les âmes
Efficace comme les mâchoires de l'hyène pour
  mastiquer les membres mal défendus des cadavres
EFFICACE
Efficace est mon action

Across seas and desert

Efficacious as coition with a young virgin
Efficacious
Efficacious as the absence of wells in the desert
Efficacious is my action
Efficacious

Efficacious as the traitor who keeps himself apart
  surrounded by his men ready to kill
Efficacious as the night for hiding things
Efficacious as the nanny-goat for producing kids
Small, small, already distressed

Efficacious as the viper
Efficacious as the knife sharpened for inflicting wounds
As the rust and urine for maintaining it
As the collisions, falls and shocks for
  enlarging it
Efficacious is my action

Efficacious as the scornful smile for raising in the chest
  of the scorned an ocean of hatred that will never dry
  up
Efficacious as the desert for dehydrating bodies and
  drying souls
Efficacious as the hyena's jaws for chewing the
  defenceless limbs of corpses
EFFICACIOUS
Efficacious is my action

Joan Peyser suggests that Boulez directs these verses against Stockhausen who had taken the leadership of the avant-garde from him. Stockhausen's new ideas were pervading the world of new music in the late fifties. His *Gruppen* for three orchestras explored spatial separation, while *Gesang der Jünglinge* (1955–56), a tape piece combining vocal and electronic sounds, constitutes one of the first compositionally successful electro–acoustic works. The element of chance also played a part in Stockhausen's work. *Je rame* has been described as a 'ritual stamping out of another person's influence',[2] and, as such, may well have expressed Boulez's feelings towards Stockhausen. There is no evidence to support this theory, however, and the object of the ritual remains a subject of speculation.

If these verses are directed by Boulez against Stockhausen in an

2. Malcolm Bowie, *Henri Michaux: A study of his literary works*, Oxford, 1973, p 115.

attempt to stamp out his influence, then why does he follow Stockhausen's lead in his setting of *Je rame* and compose a piece in which spatial separation and electronics play a part? Perhaps Boulez felt he could improve on Stockhausen's innovations in *Poésie pour pouvoir* for five-track tape and orchestra. Indeed, Boulez has criticised *Gruppen* and *Gesang der Jünglinge* for the compromises they make: 'There was a cheap side showing that I did not like very much. . .Stockhausen was covering abstract categories with splashy gowns'.[3]

Whoever was the object of Michaux's curses in Boulez's setting of *Je rame*, he or she did not have to suffer them long. *Poésie pour pouvoir* received only one performance, in October 1958 at the Donaueschingen Festival, when Otto Tomek made the following criticism: '. . .it required technical facilities that were not available at the time. . .The result was highly unsatisfactory. At that, it was fortunate the words could not be understood'.[4]

Michaux's text was committed to the tape and was treated and combined with purely electronic sounds (oscillators) and sounds taken from the orchestral part. The loudspeakers were placed behind the audience, Boulez believing that, as the loudspeaker gives nothing visually, it is necessary to turn one's back to it in order to listen to it properly. The orchestra and loudspeakers were laid out in a spiral, the orchestra starting from the floor and working up to the level of the loudspeakers, which continued the spiral to the ceiling.

The failure of *Poésie pour pouvoir* was largely due to the problem of combining a hierarchic pitch language with a tape language observing a less distinct hierarchy. Boulez feels that the two worlds have little in common or, at least, that the facility for creating an effective continuum did not exist at the time.

Boulez's turn to a longer text in *Poésie pour pouvoir* seems something of a retrogressive step in the light of the advances he made in *Le marteau*. Perhaps *Poésie pour pouvoir* was abandoned partly because it did not advance Boulez's theories of the relationship of poetry to music. Certainly, a text of this length cannot act as a 'centre and absence' like the texts of *Le marteau*.[5] It is, perhaps, surprising to find that Boulez's turn away from the poetry of his contemporary, Michaux, to the nineteenth-century poet Mallarmé, in fact constituted a progressive step.

The change of emphasis observed in *Le visage nuptial* and *Le marteau*, from a preoccupation with vocal emission to an interest in formal qualities, continues and is underlined in Boulez's settings of Mallarmé. The ideas of music as an 'irrigation' of poetry and as a 'centre and absence' attain maximum importance in these pieces. Although *Le marteau* provided Boulez with a text capable of non-

3. *B.C.C.E.*, p 136.
4. Cited by Joan Peyser in *B.C.C.E.*, p 137.
5. In his book on Boulez, Paul Griffiths tells us that a revision of *Poésie pour pouvoir* is in progress. If and when the revision appears it will be interesting to see what degree of text intelligibility is achieved and what relationship is established between the text and the music in the light of Boulez's more recent work on the shorter texts of Mallarmé and cummings.

linear development, he remained critical of Char's lack of formal awareness:

In Char and Michaux, whose works I used before coming to *Pli selon pli*, I found many sources of inspiration, but they were hardly obsessed with formal preoccupations. Char's main preoccupation is rather with the selection of an extremely pregnant vocabulary and density of expression; with Michaux it is the development of an extraordinarily original poetic imagery.[6]

What was missing from Char was not density of expression but density of form:

What attracted me in Mallarmé, at the stage I had reached at that time, was the extraordinary formal density of his poems. Not only is the content truly extraordinary – the poems possess a mythology that is very much their own – but never has the French language been taken so far in the matter of syntax.[7]

Here, Boulez mentions a further feature that divides Michaux and Char from Mallarmé. Mallarmé's progressive attitude towards syntax – the rules governing the construction of sentences – puts him in a category of artists like Joyce and Webern who 'worked on language itself'.[8] The artists who are always most important to Boulez are those who try to push language through the conventional barriers and establish new frontiers of expression:

. . .language has never been worked and forged in the same way. Mallarmé tried to rethink the foundations of French grammar. He showed this in his poems in an exceptionally condensed manner. Even his prose writings, which are no less condensed in style, and even his lectures bear the imprint of this obsession with reconstructing the French language with a slightly different syntax. This is what influenced me most in Mallarmé. I know that there is a certain preciousness that belongs to the *fin-de-siècle* outlook – I am well aware of it – but I also know that work on language has probably never been taken so far in French.[9]

Boulez's intention was to transpose Mallarmé's syntactic and formal advances into musical terms, to find a 'musical equivalent, both poetic and formal, to Mallarmé's poetry'.[10] Boulez's search for equivalents to Mallarmé's forms was not restricted to settings of Mallarmé's texts; for, following the concept of 'centre and absence', he also applied his ideas to instrumental pieces.

Stéphane Mallarmé: Un coup de dés

Boulez's contact with Mallarmé predates the setting of *Poésie pour pouvoir* by several years. The first two works to show the influence of Mallarmé were *Livre pour quatuor* (1948–49) and the *Piano sonata no. 3* (1956–57), both of which were composed before *Poésie pour pouvoir*. Both of the works were instrumental and both were strongly influenced by Mallarmé's *Un coup de dés* (A throw of the dice).

Un coup de dés is undoubtedly the most progressive and innova-

6. *C.D.*, p 93.
7. Ibid.
8. Pierre Boulez, 'Son et verbe', *R.A.*, p 58. See Chapter II.
9. *C.D.*, pp 93–94.
10. *C.D.*, p 94.

tive of Mallarmé's works. The last of his poems to be published, it represented the culmination of many of his poetic theories. *Un coup de dés* reflects the common preoccupation of poetry (especially poetry in late nineteenth-century France) with music. In *Un coup de dés*, Mallarmé attempted to create a musical score without using any of the symbols of conventional music. It is a graphic score in which the placing of the words on the paper and the size of the lettering indicate to the reader the dynamic level and pitch at which the words should be spoken. Mallarmé did not arrive at a 'musical' notation accidentally. The creation of the poem by analogy to music was quite intentional. Mallarmé made his intentions clear in a preface to the poem: '. . .cet emploi à nu de la pensée avec retraits, prolongements, fuites, ou son dessin même, résulte, pour qui veut lire à haute voix, une partition.' (. . .this unadorned use of thought with doublings back, goings on, runnings away, or the very portrayal of it, results, for who will read aloud, in a musical score.)[11] At the end of this preface, Mallarmé reclaims for literature certain aspects of music in much the same way as Boulez claims for music certain aspects of literature:[12] '. . .Musique. . .on en retrouve plusieurs moyens m'ayant semblé appartentir aux Lettres, je les reprends.' (. . .Music. . .several means we rediscovered from it which have seemed to me to belong to Letters, I take them back.)[13]

The white spaces that separate the words in *Un coup de dés* represent silence and, as in Webern's music, this silence is to be enjoyed as much as the music. The double lines, which occur naturally where the two pages of a book meet, represent the musical staff. Each double page is a unit or bar. The words are arranged so that one reads down and across the double page. Tempo is determined by the amount of words on a page. If there is only one word on a page, the reader is invited to dwell on that word: if there are several words, then he will read through them more quickly. Dynamics are determined by the weight of the typeface and pitch is governed by the placing of the word on the page – intonation will rise towards the centre of the page and fall towards the end. Motifs are unified by the use of the same typeface. For example, the words '*Un coup de dés jamais n'abolira le hasard*' (A dice throw will never do away with chance) appear in isolated places on different pages, but are unified as a sentence by their being printed in the largest case. Finally, a sort of counterpoint is achieved by the placing of divergent ideas around what Mallarmé calls the *fil conducteur*, the central theme. It is also possible for a reader to experience a 'chordal' presentation of themes by looking at a page and seeing its ideas not consecutively but simultaneously.

Of course, Mallarmé was not only concerned with the musical sound and presentation of his poem but, also, with the sense. *Un*

11. Mallarmé's preface to *Un coup de dés*, tr. Keith Bosley in *Mallarmé, The poems*, London, 1977, pp 254–55.
12. 'I demand for music the right to parentheses and italics. . .', Pierre Boulez, 'Recherches maintenant', *R.A.*, p 32.
13. Mallarmé, op. cit, pp 256–57.

coup de dés combines many of the most important symbols and themes of Mallarmé's work. The central images of *Un coup de dés* are of the sun, the sky, a ship, and its voyage and shipwreck. The image of the voyage is used, like that of flight, as a metaphor for poetic creation. The poet's voyage leads him away from comfort and security into a world where he will be subject to the vagaries of chance. The star becomes the poet's guide; the tempest, the poetic struggle; and the shipwreck, the ever-present threat of failure. The symbols used in *Un coup de dés* had been rigorously developed by Mallarmé in earlier poems. *Le vierge, le vivace et le bel aujourd'hui* and *À la nue accablante tu* described the poetic process in terms of a 'flight' and a voyage respectively. In *Un coup de dés*, these symbols merge and the ship's sail is described as a hopelessly flapping wing.

Un coup de dés was a truly prophetic work. Its typographical mimesis (the layout of the words suggesting at times the ship's voyage and at others the constellation of stars) looks forward to the work of the Concrete poets. The intention to create a musical score without reference to conventional notation looks forward to more recent experiments in notational techniques. Perhaps the most prophetic aspect of *Un coup de dés* was its preoccupation with chance. Not only is chance one of the central themes of the poem, but the text achieves a polyvalence of reading possibilities. In reading *Un coup de dés*, the eye can follow several routes among the words. There was to be a similar element of variable form in much music of the nineteen-fifties and sixties and, in Boulez's case, the model of *Un coup de dés* was *directly* responsible for his introduction and development of this idea.

In his article of 1954, 'Recherches maintenant', Boulez suggests that musical works should seek non-linear types of development and demanded for music the right to parentheses and italics.[14] In a later article, 'Sonate, que me veux-tu?', he claimed that a lingua franca of modern music had been established and that the composer must now turn his attention to the question of form. Boulez argued that form should be as flexible as the new language and should be integrated with it:

. . .music currently possesses a broad range of means, a vocabulary which once again attains universality of conception and comprehension. Admittedly, this equipment still requires a great deal of improvement and must be given time to be broken in, acquire more flexibility, become standard. Nevertheless, the essential discoveries have been made, the direction has been ineluctably taken and we have before us a certain margin of safety when it comes to composing, stylistically speaking. But one major job remains: the notion of form must be reconsidered from top to bottom. It is obvious that in dealing with an increasingly aperiodic asymmetric vocabulary and a constantly evolving morphology, one cannot apply formal criteria that have a reference basis without making them lose all value and depriving them of coherence. The task of placing the formal possibilities of music

14. Pierre Boulez, 'Recherches maintenant', *R.A.*, p 32.

on an equal footing with morphology and syntax seems more and more urgent; fluidity of form must integrate fluidity of vocabulary.[15]

Boulez, then, was seeking alternatives to the standard predetermined linear forms of Western music. The beginnings of the move away from such linear progressions can be seen in *Le marteau*, where he adopted Char's archipelago technique. In *Le marteau*, however, the sequence of movements was fixed. The next step was to allow variable progressions through a piece, allowing the performer to choose the sequence of movements or passages. Boulez described the process in terms of a labyrinth, where one can always choose new routes: '...the work must provide a certain number of possible routes...with chance playing a shunting role at the last moment.'[16] Here, we can see the influence of *Un coup de dés*, where there is often more than one possible sequence of images, more than one possible route through the words.

The first piece to be influenced by these ideas was *Livre pour quatuor* of 1948–49. Initially, this piece was to consist of detachable movements from which the players would choose which ones they wanted to play:

The idea of a *Livre* for string quartet, which, right from the start, was to be made up of detachable movements, came to me in 1948/49, probably while reading *Igitur*[17] and *Un Coup de Dés*. I had found that the poem was no longer an isolated fragment, but that it might be part of a wide continuity as well as one that could be broken up: in other words, a continuity from which sections could be detached because they had meaning and validity even when taken out of the continuous context in which they were placed. That is what interested me.[18]

In its finished version, however, the quartet had three fixed movements. Later still Boulez made the quartet into a two-movement piece for string orchestra.

If *Livre pour quatuor* was influenced only in a vague way by *Un coup de dés*, and the techniques it suggests were not carried through in a thorough way, it was quite otherwise with the *Piano sonata no. 3* of 1956–57. In his article 'Sonate, que me veux-tu?', Boulez describes the sonata as a 'work in progress' – a description he borrows from Joyce, who gave this title to passages of *Finnegans Wake* which were published before the work was completed. The five movements of this piece, of which only three have been completed, can be played in one of eight orders. The pieces are arranged in the form of a constellation around the central *Constellation / Constellation miroir*:

...around the central core (which is itself a grouping of cells) gravitate the four formants grouped two by two in concentric orbits; the exterior orbit may become interior, and vice versa. This creates eight possibilities of performance in all, given the symmetrical requirements that the permutations must satisfy [Example 35].[19]

The idea of organising a text in the form of a constellation, like the

15. Pierre Boulez, 'Sonate, que me veux-tu?', *Perspectives of New Music*, i, 2 (1963), p 33.
16. Ibid, p 35.
17. *Igitur* is an early prose poem that Mallarmé left unfinished.
18. *C.D.*, pp 50–51.
19. Pierre Boulez, 'Sonate, que me veux-tu?', *Perspectives of New Music*, i, 2 (1963), p 43.

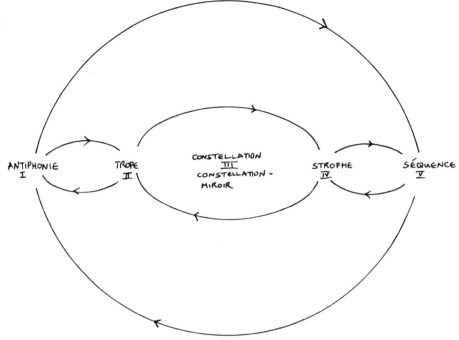

Example 35

idea of guided chance, derives from *Un coup de dés*, where Mallarmé aimed to achieve such an arrangement of words:

The poem is being printed at this very moment, just as I conceived it regarding pagination, in which lies the whole effect...The constellation will inevitably suggest, according to exact laws and to the extent that a printed page can do so, the look of a constellation.[20]

The concept of the constellation is important in Boulez's *Piano sonata no. 3*. It defines the overall structure of the piece and influences the compositional procedure of *Constellation / Constellation miroir*. This piece, the central movement of the sonata, is reversible. On one page, one finds the original form (*Constellation*); on the other its retrograde sequel (*Miroir*). The piece is in mirror form because of its immovable place in the middle of the sonata: it can be approached from either side, the *Constellation* may be followed by its mirror image or the mirror image may precede the *Constellation*. The text is written in two colours, reflecting Mallarmé's preoccupation with typography. The groups in green Boulez describes as *points* and those in red as *blocs*. The groups in green contain isolated pitches, with chords only resulting from the coincidence of points. The groups in red contain chords or blocks of sound. Green and red groups are alternated in the order in which they appear. A great many routes may be taken within each group

20. Cited by Pierre Boulez, ibid., p 41.

and, at the end of each line, there are directions which tell the player how to get from one line to another. Some of the directions are optional, others are mandatory.

> . . .within each group there is a great diversity of routes. . .at the beginning or at the end of each line there are reference signs which indicate the way to pass from one line to another, and, when necessary, the consequences that that implies in the duration (tempo susceptible to *modifications* while proceeding, or radically different but stable) and in the dynamics. Certain directions are obligatory, others optional, but *everything* must be played. In some ways, this *Constellation* is like the map of an unknown city (which plays so large a role in *L'Emploi du temps*, by Michel Butor). The itinerary is left to the interpreter's initiative, he must direct himself through a tight network of routes. This form, which is both fixed and mobile, is situated, because of this ambiguity, in the centre of the work for which it serves as a pivot, as a centre of gravity.[21]

The relation of Boulez's *Constellation* in the *Piano sonata no. 3* to Mallarmé's constellation technique in *Un coup de dés* is fairly obvious. While Mallarmé leaves to the reader the route to be taken between words and images, and guides choice by the placing of words, Boulez provides written instructions indicating the transition between musical ideas.

Each of the five movements of the sonata provides a different balance between choice and predetermination. In the first movement, *Antiphonie*, the only variable is the overall plan. The music is written on separate sheets which can be arranged in four different orders. Boulez's procedure here is paralleled by Mallarmé's approach in *Le livre*, a book for which he left notes but which he did not complete:

> I had completed most of my task when there appeared a book containing Mallarmé's posthumous notes written for the work called *Le livre* which he was planning. . .This was a revelation to me, and I use the word in its strongest sense. My deliberation and the goals that I had set for myself after *Un Coup de Dés* coincided with the very aims that Mallarmé had pursued and formulated, although he did not have time enough to conclude his investigations.[22]

Mallarmé's *Livre*, made entirely of loose leaves, was to be both book and album: the pages could be read successively, as one reads an ordinary book, or each leaf could be considered independently. The leaves of the book could then be reassembled and reconstructed in any order. *Le livre* was not to be a personal statement but an objective one, treating the totality of things, a work not expressing the identity of its author but reflecting the patterns of nature, a work already written 'au folio du ciel'.[23] Mallarmé's plans for the work were more concerned with its overall structure than with its content. He formulated structural principles that would be valid at all levels of the composition, principles permitting permutation of the components and allowing mobility within this framework. It is

21. Pierre Boulez, ibid., p 41.
22. Ibid, p 36.
23. Stéphane Mallarmé, 'Crayonné au théâtre', *Oeuvres complètes*, p 294.

exactly this idea of formal principles governing global and local aspects of the composition and permitting mobility and renewability which one finds in the *Piano sonata no. 3*.

The ideas contained in *Le livre* were an extension of the ideas of *Un coup de dés*. Mallarmé's ideals were realised by Boulez in the *Piano sonata no. 3*, not through an imitation of Mallarmé's unfinished project, but by an independent extension of the ideas of *Un coup de dés*. Here, one encounters the remarkable phenomenon of poetry leaning towards music, in Mallarmé's attempts to create a poem with elements of musical notation, and music leaning towards poetry, in Boulez's attempt to adopt Mallarmé's non-linear forms and typographical innovations, the ideals of one form finally reaching fruition in the other.

In the second movement, *Trope*, there is a greater degree of indeterminacy than in the opening movement, but not as much as in *Constellation / Constellation Miroir*. The four sections of the movement are arranged in cyclic form and, in this respect, *Trope* represents a microcosm of the global form. The titles of the sections of the movement are taken from the terminology of literary criticism, *texte*, *parenthèse*, *commentaire*, *glose*, titles which Boulez tells us are 'related words, almost synonymous, indicating the very slight differences among the tropes'.[24] The player takes any of the sections as a starting point. This basic principle is complicated by the inclusion of duplicate copies of *commentaire*: one is situated between *parenthèse* and *glose*, the other between *texte* and *glose*. The player will play only one of these.

The last two movements have not reached a definitive state. *Strophe* is being adapted to Mallarmé's idea of the 'thickness' of a book as a guide to form: the further one penetrates a book the more complicated and evolved are the ideas, and one reads page thirty in a different way from page one. The piece will consist of four strophes. Each strophe will increase in size as each section will incorporate the previous ones. The sequence of the strophes is not fixed, however, so there can be many possible permutations. Whatever the sequence of movements, the principle of increasing 'thickness' will be observed.

The final piece, to be called *Séquence*, will contain the largest degree of indeterminacy. Boulez tells us, however, that 'the variability' he seeks is 'incompatible with notation as it is used at the present time'. It seems that Boulez has not yet found a solution to the notational problem it poses.

Piano sonata no. 3 provides the clearest example of poetry 'irrigating' music and acting on it as a 'centre and absence'. In it, we see Boulez explicitly searching for musical equivalents to poetry. *Piano sonata no. 3* illustrates one of the most sophisticated ways in

24. Pierre Boulez, 'Sonate, que me veux-tu?', *Perspectives of New Music*, i, 2 (1963), p 39.

which music can react to poetry. Lesser intellects inspired by *Un coup de dés* would, perhaps, have set the poem for voices, turning the implied musical elements of Mallarmé's poem into musical terms. Boulez's approach is much more subtle. Seeing the underlying idea of *Un coup de dés* as an inclination of one art form to another, he 'sets' the poem in a similar way, writing music that inclines to poetry. *Piano sonata no. 3* is a most striking example of the interpenetration of art forms, Boulez fulfilling in musical terms Mallarmé's literary ambitions.

Structures – deuxième livre

In the second book of *Structures*, written between 1956 and 1961, Boulez's literary orientation is still clearly discernible. The two movements of the work are called *chapitres* and sections of the second chapter are referred to as *textes* and *encarts*.[25]

The particular literary influence is still that of Joyce and Mallarmé. As in *Piano sonata no. 3*, their influence underlies the use of polyvalent form. Although the first chapter is fully notated and, therefore, follows a 'simple trajectory', the second chapter requires the performer to choose between various *pièces*, *textes* and *encarts*, in a form that is conceived according to the labyrinthine principles developed in *Piano sonata no. 3*. The presentation of the music – several sheets contained in a folio – is once more reminiscent of Mallarmé's idea of *Le livre*.

The music of *Structures – deuxième livre* is improvisatory in style. Passages are often marked *libre* and are subject to constant fluctuation of tempo, while pauses and *appoggiaturas* serve to obscure the sense of metre. There is a clear contrast between the first and the second chapters: in the first chapter, the style sounds improvisatory, although everything is notated; in the second chapter, performer decisions are called for. Thus, the piece moves from determinacy to indeterminacy, Boulez ably incorporating the new literary-derived principles of polyvalence and indeterminacy into his compositional technique

Pli selon pli: portrait de Mallarmé.

That Mallarmé is one of the most important artists to have influenced Boulez is established unequivocally in Boulez's large-scale tribute to the nineteenth-century symbolist poet, entitled *Pli selon pli: portrait de Mallarmé*.

As with *Piano sonata no. 3*, Boulez treated *Pli selon pli* as a 'work in progress', presenting movements individually. Unlike *Piano sonata no. 3*, the five movements of *Pli selon pli* have all been

25. The word used in bookbinding circles to describe extra pages inserted into a book.

finished, although pieces have been subject to revision, as is often the case with Boulez. The five movements were written between the years 1957 and 1962. The titles of the movements follow, in the order in which they appear in the work:

1 *Don*
2 *Improvisation sur Mallarmé: Le vierge, le vivace et le bel aujourd'hui*
3 *Improvisation sur Mallarmé: Une dentelle s'abolit*
4 *Improvisation sur Mallarmé: À la nue accablante tu*
5 *Tombeau.*

The outer movements are for soprano and large orchestra, with extensive batteries of percussion. The three *Improvisations* are for soprano, with more modest ensembles dominated by percussion instruments, tuned and untuned. The first *Improvisation* has been revised since its publication in 1958. In the revised version, wind, brass and strings support the percussion instruments, reinforcing phrases or adding sustained sounds. The second *Improvisation* uses percussion instruments with piano and harp. The third *Improvisation* uses percussion instruments of the orchestra in a similar way to the revised version of the first *Improvisation*. Despite the use of orchestral instruments in the first and third *Improvisations*, the contrast between the larger ensembles of the outer movements and the smaller ensembles of the *Improvisations* is preserved: 'The two outer pieces call for a relatively large ensemble producing an orchestral sound; the three central pieces more nearly approach chamber music, both in writing and sonority, particularly the second sonnet: *Une dentelle s'abolit*.'[26]

In *Piano sonata no. 3*, Boulez took the idea of poetry as a 'centre and absence' of music to its logical conclusion. In it, we witnessed the unique and remarkable phenomenon of poetry defining the musical conception without the poem itself being sung or intoned in any way. In *Pli selon pli*, Boulez combined this new type of 'setting' with a more conventional approach. The first movement of *Pli selon pli* uses only the first line of Mallarmé's *Don du poëme*: 'Je t'apporte l'enfant d'une nuit d'Idumée!'. This line is set at the very start of the movement. *Le vierge, le vivace et le bel aujourd'hui* and *Une dentelle s'abolit* are set in full, but only the first three lines of *À la nue accablante tu* appear in the score. In the last movement, Boulez sets only the last line of Mallarmé's epitaph for Verlaine, *Tombeau*: 'Un peu profond ruisseau calomnié la mort.' This line is set at the very end of the movement. There are, therefore, two ways of treating the text. Either a fragment of the text is used epigrammatically at the start or close of a movement, or the text is set in its entirety. In addition to these two basic techniques, Boulez

26. From Boulez's note to his 1969 Columbia recording of *Pli selon pli*.

superimposes fragments of the three improvisations over the orchestral texture of *Don*. This could be considered as a third technique or approach to the text.

The title *Pli selon pli* is taken from Mallarmé's poem, *Remémoration d'amis belges*, in which he describes the grey stone of the city of Bruges appearing 'fold by fold' as dawn breaks. The poem is not set to music in any way, the title only being used to describe the work:

> The title – *Pli selon pli* – is taken from a Mallarmé poem not used in my musical transposition; it indicates the meaning and direction of the work. In this poem the author thus describes the way in which the dissolving mist gradually reveals the stones of the city of Bruges. In the same way as the five pieces unfold, they reveal, fold by fold, a portrait of Mallarmé.[27]

This could be considered as a fourth category in Boulez's use of poetry in a musical setting.

The four categories represent the extremes between conventional setting, and setting as a 'centre and absence'. In the outer movements, the relation of the poetry to the music is established in the most economical way. The singer presents one line only, the music acting on the poetry as a 'centre and absence'.

Although the texts used in the central *Improvisations* are largely complete (the full texts are used in *Le vierge, le vivace et le bel aujourd'hui* and in *Une dentelle s'abolit*, and the first three lines in *À la nue accablante tu*), an opposition between direct and indirect understanding remains. At times, the words can be understood; at other times, the words are treated as a raw material for musical elaboration and here the style of setting moves towards the category of 'centre and absence'. In *Don*, where fragments of the *Improvisations* are used completely out of context, the use of the text as a raw material is most clearly observed. The phrase *pli selon pli* in the title is a rather unusual case of the use of poetry in a musical context. Boulez's setting cannot be said to be about the poem from which it is taken, although, as Boulez says, the phrase does indicate 'the meaning and direction of the work'[28] as a whole.

The contrasted styles of treatment of the text help to establish the form of the work, the outer movements in 'epigrammatic' style, and two of the inner movements. The symmetrical, five-movement plan is further reinforced by the instrumentation, the epigrammatic movements using large orchestra while the inner movements use smaller ensembles. The smallest ensemble is found at the centre of the work. The direction, then, is from epigrammatic setting to complete setting and back to epigrammatic setting; from full orchestral setting to chamber ensemble and back to full orchestral setting (Example 36). Like many forms in Boulez, the plan is highly symmetrical.[29] The form of *Piano sonata no. 3*, where the movements are arranged in concentric circles around *Constellation /*

27. Ibid.
28. Ibid.
29. *Pli selon pli* did not originally possess this degree of symmetry. Paul Griffiths points out that, in its first performance in 1960, *Don* was merely a piano piece after Mallarmé's *Don du poème*, and so the music made a large *crescendo*, moving from the opening piano version of *Don*, through the 'chamber' music of the central *Improvisations* to the orchestral setting of *Tombeau*. Paul Griffiths, *Boulez*, London, 1978, p 45.

1 <u>DON</u>	ORCHESTRA AND VOICE ↓ ORCHESTRA	EPIGRAMMATIC SETTING
2 <u>LE VIERGE, LE VIVACE</u>	ORCHESTRAL INSTRUMENTS, PERCUSSION AND VOICE	SETTING OF FULL TEXT
3 <u>UNE DENTELLE S'ABOLIT</u>	PERCUSSION, HARP AND VOICE	
4 <u>A LA NUE ACCABLANTE TU</u>	ORCHESTRAL INSTRUMENTS, PERCUSSION AND VOICE	SETTING OF PART OF TEXT
5 <u>TOMBEAU</u>	ORCHESTRA ↓ ORCHESTRA AND VOICE	EPIGRAMMATIC SETTING

Example 36

Constellation miroir, displayed a comparable symmetry, despite its element of indeterminacy. A more direct comparison could be made with the form of some movements in *Le marteau* (see Chapter III).

The five poems Boulez drew on in *Pli selon pli* were not composed as a cycle by Mallarmé. All of the poems, with the exception of *Don du poëme*, date from Mallarmé's mature years (c.1882–98). *Don du poëme* was written in the period of Mallarmé's early manhood (c.1862–65), the period in which he composed *L'après-midi d'un faune*, which is, in many ways, an impressionist rather than a symbolist work. Here are the five sonnets in the order in which they appear in *Pli selon pli*. The full text of the first, fourth and last poems is provided.

Don du poëme

Je t'apporte l'enfant d'une nuit d'Idumée!
Noire, à l'aile saignante et pâle, déplumée,
Par le verre brûlé d'aromates et d'or,
Par les carreaux glacés, hélas! mornes encore,
L'aurore se jeta sur la lampe angélique.
Palmes! et quand elle a montré cette relique
À ce père essayant un sourire ennemi,
La solitude bleue et stérile a frémi.
Ô la berceuse, avec ta fille et l'innocence
De vos pieds froids, accueille une horrible naissance:
Et ta voix rappelant viole et clavecin,
Avec le doigt fané presseras-tu le sein
Par qui coule en blancheur sibylline la femme
Pour les lèvres que l'air du vierge azur affame?

*

Le vierge, le vivace et le bel aujourd'hui
Va-t-il nous déchirer avec un coup d'aile ivre
Ce lac dur oublié que hante sous le givre
Le transparent glacier des vols qui n'ont pas fui!

Un cygne d'autrefois se souvient que c'est lui
Magnifique mais qui sans espoir se délivre
Pour n'avoir pas chanté la région où vivre
Quand du stérile hiver a resplendi l'ennui.

Tout son col secouera cette blanche agonie
Par l'espace infligée à l'oiseau qui le nie,
Mais non l'horreur du sol où le plumage est pris.

Fantôme qu'à ce lieu son pur éclat assigne,
Il s'immobilise au songe froid de mépris
Que vêt parmi l'exil inutile le Cygne.

*

Une dentelle s'abolit
Dans le doute du Jeu suprême
À n'entr'ouvrir comme un blasphème
Qu'absence éternelle de lit.

Cet unanime blanc conflit
D'une guirlande avec la même,
Enfui contre la vitre blême
Flotte plus qu'il n'ensevelit.

Mais, chez qui du rêve se dore
Tristement dort une mandore
Au creux néant musicien

Telle que vers quelque fenêtre
Selon nul ventre que le sien,
Filial on aurait pu naître.

*

Gift of the poem

I bring you the child of an Edomitish night!
Black, its wing bleeding and pale, featherless,
Through the burnt glass of gold and spices,
Through the frozen windows, alas! still gloomy,
The dawn threw itself on the angelic lamp.
Palms! and when it showed this relic
To this father trying a hostile smile,
The blue and sterile solitude shook.
Oh lullaby, with your daughter and innocence
With your cold feet, welcome a horrible birth:
And your voice recalling viol and harpsichord,
Will you squeeze with your faded finger the breast
Where flows the woman in oracular whiteness
For lips starved by the virgin blue?

*

The virginal, irrepressible and beautiful day
Will it tear for us with one stroke of its drunken wing
This hard forgotten lake haunted beneath the frost
By the transparent glacier of flights unflown!

A swan of yesteryear remembers that it is he
Magnificent but who without hope frees himself
For not having sung of the region in which to live
When the boredom of sterile winter has shone forth.

His whole neck will shake off this white agony
Inflicted by space on the bird who denies it,
But not the horror of the earth where his plumage is
    caught.

Phantom assigned to this place by his pure radiance,
Stilled in the cold dream of contempt
Which clothes the swan in his useless exile.

*

A piece of lace is abolished
In doubt of the supreme Game
Half-opening like a blasphemy
Only the eternal absence of bed

The unanimous white conflict
Of a garland with its like,
Vanishing against the pale glass
Floating more than burying.

But, in him who gilds himself with dream
Sadly a mandola sleeps
In the hollow musical void

Such that towards some window
By no womb but its own,
Filial one might have been born.

*

À la nue accablante tu
Basse de basalte et de laves
À même les échos esclaves
Par une trompe sans vertu

Quel sépulcral naufrage (tu
Le sais, écume, mais y baves)
Suprême une entre les épaves
Abolit le mât dévêtu

Ou cela que furibond faute
De quelque perdition haute
Tout l'abîme vain éployé

Dans le si blanc cheveu qui traîne
Avarement aura noyé
Le flanc enfant d'une sirène.

To the overwhelming skies hushed
Bass of basalt and lava
Even to the enslaved echoes
By a virtueless horn

What sepulchral shipwreck (you
Know it foam, but slaver there)
Supreme piece among the wreckage
Abolished the sailless mast

Or that which furious for want
Of some high perdition
The whole vain abyss loosed

In such white trailing hair
Avariciously will have drowned
A siren's young flank.

Tombeau

ANNIVERSAIRE – JANVIER 1897

Le noir roc courroucé que la bise le roule
Ne s'arrêtera ni sous de pieuses mains
Tâtant sa ressemblance avec les maux humains
Comme pour en bénir quelque funeste moule.

Ici presque toujours si le ramier roucoule
Cet immatériel deuil opprime de maints
Nubiles plis l'astre mûri des lendemains
Dont un scintillement argentera la foule.

Qui cherche, parcourant le solitaire bond
Tantôt extérieur de notre vagabond –
Verlaine? Il est caché parmi l'herbe, Verlaine

À ne surprendre que naïvement d'accord
La lèvre sans y boire ou tarir son haleine
Un peu profond ruisseau calomnié la mort.

Tomb

ANNIVERSARY – JANUARY 1897

The black rock angry that the north wind rolls it
Will not stop even under pious hands
Feeling for the resemblance with human ills
As if to bless some fateful mould.

Here almost always if the ringdove coos
The immaterial grief oppresses by many nubile folds
The ripened star of tomorrows
Whose gleam will silver the crowd.

Who seeks, traversing the lonely bound,
Once outside, of our vagabond –
Verlaine? He is hidden in the grass, Verlaine

Only to surprise in simple agreement
Without his lips drinking or his breath drying up
A shallow and slandered river, death.

Why, one wonders, did Boulez choose these five poems to make a portrait of Mallarmé? Hidden within their mazy syntax and obscure imagery must be some link or common factor.

The outer poems are connected in the most direct way. *Don du poëme* describes a birth and *Tombeau* describes a death. Boulez's portrait, therefore, opens and closes, like most biographies, with birth and death. Admittedly, the birth described in *Don du poëme* is not Mallarmé's birth, but the birth of a poem; and the death described in *Tombeau* is not Mallarmé's death but Verlaine's. But, following the spirit of symbolist poetry, we are justified in regarding the opening and closing lines, as they are used by Boulez, as describing Mallarmé's birth and death. This is one level of interpretation – one fold of meaning.

Boulez identifies with Mallarmé in many ways: their preoccupations are similar, both have 'worked on language', both are greatly concerned with form and purity of style. The child that Boulez brings us in *Pli selon pli* is Boulez himself as much as Mallarmé. *Pli selon pli* is as much autobiography as biography. This is a second level of interpretation – a second fold of meaning.

But the birth the opening poem describes is not a happy one. The child had Edom's night for a mother and 'the child of Edom was the country of Esau, the brother disinherited in favour of Jacob'.[30] So the child is not only *saignante et pâle* but also disinherited. The Edomitish night may, also, refer to Edom's battles for freedom. In this respect, Mallarmé refers to the battle of creation, which is really the central theme of the poem. The opening image of the poem gains in potency when one remembers that Mallarmé would often work through the night, a poem being the product of a night's work. Mallarmé's critical sense causes him to disinherit his poetic progeny whose wing is *saignante et pâle*. 'Wing' is used here as a symbol of poetic flight. The poem is bleeding from the trauma of poetic creation, having been plucked through *les carreaux glacés* of poetic sterility. In the following poems, whiteness and ice, symbols of the struggle against poetic sterility, emerge as the principal symbols of the poems, as Boulez has arranged them. The lines, then, describe the birth of a poem, an unsatisfactory birth but, nevertheless, a birth. In describing the particular, Mallarmé refers to the universal. 'This child' is not just one of Mallarmé's poems but all of his poems; and *Don du poëme*, therefore, describes Mallarmé's complete *oeuvre*. *Pli selon pli* is a portrait of Mallarmé through his poetry. This is a third level of interpretation – a third fold of meaning (Example 37).

The important ice/white symbol of *Don du poëme* is taken up in the first full setting, *Le vierge, le vivace et le bel aujourd'hui*, which presents an image of a swan frozen in a hard, forgotten lake. The ice

30. Wallace Fowlie, cited by Joan Peyser in *B.C.C.E.*, p 141.

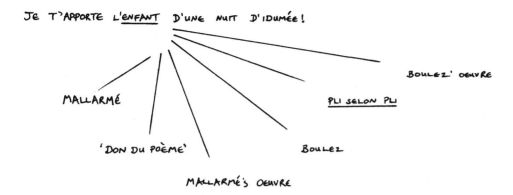

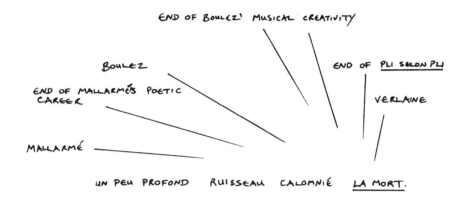

Example 37

restricts flight – will the pure and beautiful day be able to free the swan? Another important symbol carried forward from *Don du poëme* is the symbol of flight which describes poetic flight. The swan, or poet, suffers *blanche agonie*, the agony of sterility. The whiteness that is the poet's enemy is the whiteness of the paper that faces him at the start of a creative venture. The swan will not escape completely from this 'white agony'; he will still be tied to the earth – 'caught by his plumage'. The poet is similarly exiled from ordinary life, caught in a forgotten lake, making unsuccessful attempts to poetic flight, his wings flapping hopelessly in the water below the ice.[31] As with the opening poem, *Le vierge, le vivace et le bel aujourd'hui* probably describes Boulez as much as Mallarmé.

The theme of poetic struggle is carried through all five poems. The *Jeu suprême* of *Une dentelle s'abolit* may refer to such a contention for poetic heights; the *absence éternelle de lit* may refer again to Mallarmé's night labour, and the *blanc conflit* is certainly a reference to the struggle against poetic sterility. The colour white

31. The symbol of the swan in exile, describing the poet's predicament, is not a new one. Baudelaire's *Le cygne* describes a swan exiled in a city, trapped not in ice but in stone.

occurs in a less obvious context in *À la nue accablante tu*, where the knowing 'foam' (implicitly an element of whiteness) covers the tomb of the wreck. This sonnet exchanges the symbol of poetic 'flight' of *Le vierge, le vivace et le bel aujourd'hui* for that of the poetic 'voyage'. The theme of *À la nue accablante tu* is very close to that of *Un coup de dès*, where white foam symbolises the impending poetic failure, as it threatens to engulf the poetic project. White is implied through its antithesis at the start of *Tombeau*, where the 'black rock' refers to Verlaine's tomb and, symbolically, to the end of poetic creation.

Other recurrent images reinforce the central theme of poetic creation. One such set of images which would have increased the significance of these poems for Boulez is the repeated reference to musical instruments. In *Don du poëme*, a mother's voice is compared to the sound of harpsichord and viol. The mother here is not so much a mother of mortals as a mother of creation. In *Une dentelle s'abolit*, we are told that he who has gilded dreams will not draw sounds from his mandola or combat the hollow, musical void and fulfil his musical potential. Perhaps the *trompe sans vertu* in *À la nue accablante tu* restricts creation in a similar way. The idea that a lack of virtue restricts poetic effort is implied in *Le vierge, le vivace et le bel aujourd'hui*, where the poet hopes that these elements of purity will combine to free the swan.

These are just a few of the important symbols contained in these five poems. It would not be possible or appropriate to examine all of the symbols of the poems in this study. The prime significance of the poems for Boulez having been established, attention must now focus on the musical treatment of the chosen texts.

Boulez's intention in *Pli selon pli*, as with *Piano sonata no. 3*, was to find musical equivalents to Mallarmé's poetry. He felt that there were various possible levels of convergence of poetry and music. The first level at which poetry and music may converge is the poetic one:

> There are various levels of convergence. The simplest and most emotional is the poetic one which I tried to achieve by using certain equivalent sonorities. Thus when Mallarmé uses words like 'green', 'white', 'absence', and so on, there is after all a certain sonority in music that is directly associated with such ideas – for instance, certain extremely long-held, extremely tense sounds, which form part of this sort of universe that is not so much frozen as extraordinarily 'vitrified'. It was this emotional, direct level that made me select certain poems rather than others. It was not simply because he wrote sonnets that I chose Mallarmé's poetry, but because it had a very precise meaning for me.[32]

Boulez identifies the colour white, and the idea of absence, as important symbols in the poems. Moreover, these important symbols have direct musical equivalents. Examples of sustained, tense

32. *C.D.*, pp 94–95.

sounds are not difficult to find in *Pli selon pli*. The opening of *Le vierge, le vivace et le bel aujourd'hui*, where the white–frost–sterility symbol is most prominent, is dominated by such sounds. The vibraphone has repeated chords, containing the minor ninth and the major seventh, both inversions of the semitone (Example 38). The rest of the ensemble contribute brittle percussion sounds (metal blocks, castanets, gongs, harp). Indeed, the whole setting is characterised by long-held sounds suggesting whiteness and absence.

Don, which introduces the cycle, opens with a striking ice/white musical symbol. Here an initial, loud burst of sound gives way to a long, tense string chord (Example 39). Does this opening burst describe the birth of the child of Edom, brought 'Through the burnt glass of gold and spices'? Anthony Cross describes it as 'a very traditional call to attention in that its function is, by contrast, to emphasise the following stillness, thereby focusing attention on the voice's "syllabic declamation".'[33] Cross's description is certainly accurate, but it does not take into account the descriptive or poetic significance of the sound. In the opening bars of *Don*, the orchestra is divided into three groups, according to register (high, middle, low).[34] These superimposed folds of sound, possibly representing the 'folds' referred to in the title, make much of the sort of tense, attenuated sound that Boulez describes as 'white'.

The second *Improvisation*, *Une dentelle s'abolit*, like the first, contains so many long-held and tense sounds that it is hard to point to one single area to illustrate Boulez's descriptive or poetic use of sound. The piano sonorities that accompany the words *blanc conflit*, however, illustrate the point as well as any other. The brittle tense sounds of the piano underline in musical terms the whiteness of poetic conflict (Example 40). Like the first *Improvisation*, the overall tone colour produced by the ensemble in *Une dentelle s'abolit* (harp, tubular bells, vibraphone, piano, celesta and percussion) has an icy sheen.

Boulez does not only seek equivalents for Mallarmé's poetry on the descriptive level. Characteristically, his attention turns also to the question of form:

This is why I chose very strict forms from Mallarmé in order to graft on to them a proliferation of music sprouting from an equally strict form; this enabled me to transcribe into musical terms forms that I had never thought of and which are derived from the literary forms he himself used. . .These *Improvisations* become an analysis of the sonnet structure, in a more and more detailed and more and more profound way. This is why I called them *Improvisations I, II, III*. The first takes a sonnet and uncovers only its strophic character, which is not very intense work; the second is elaborated at the level of the line and verse itself – in other words, it is already an analysis of the stanza; the third proceeds in the sense that the line itself has a particular structure in terms of its position within the sonnet.[35]

33. Anthony Cross, 'Form and expression in Boulez's *Don*', *Music Review*, xxxvi (1975), p 216.
34. The principle underlying the organisation of the groups of the orchestra is pointed out by Anthony Cross, ibid., p 217.
35. *C.D.*, pp 94–95.

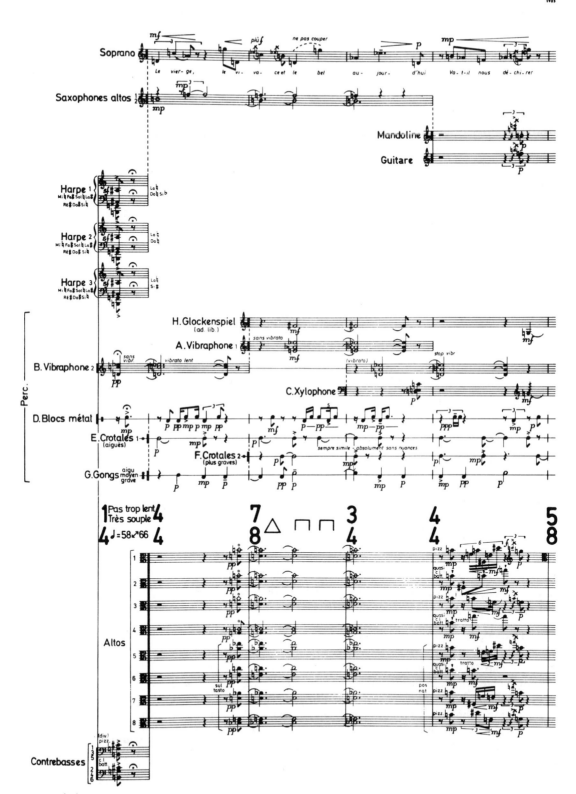

Example 38

don

pierre boulez

Universal Edition Nr. 13614 LW

Example 39

Senza tempo

Example 40

Le vierge, le vivace et le bel aujourd'hui provides the clearest example of the composer adopting Mallarmé's form. The singing in each stanza is mostly continuous, each stanza being separated by an instrumental interlude. The contrast between voice setting and instrumental sections reveals the strophic structure. To highlight the contrast between vocal and instrumental sections, and to clarify the form, each section is given a different tempo. The tempos vary between *modéré* and *très lent*. The music has a concentric form of seven sections: the instrumentation emphasises the symmetry of form, the first and third interludes being dominated by vibraphone, while the central section involves all the players.

1 *Pas trop lent*	————————	
2 *Modéré*	inst. interlude	vibraphone
3 *Très Modéré*	————————	
4 *Très lent*	inst. interlude	ensemble
5 *Pas trop lent*	————————	
6 *Modéré*	inst. interlude	vibraphone
7 *Pas trop lent*	————————	
(8) (*Très lent*)	(coda)	(ensemble)

(The lines refer to stanzas of the poem)

Here we see the coincidence of a strict musical form (Boulez's favourite, concentric, form) with a strict literary form (Mallarmé's favourite, sonnet, form). They are not in conflict, however. The two forms are integrated, the graft of music and poetry enabling Boulez to 'transcribe into musical terms' forms that he had 'never thought of and which were derived from literary forms Mallarmé himself used'.[36]

In the second *Improvisation*, we are told that the music is 'elaborated at the level of the line and verse itself'. Boulez does this by using the 'numerical relationships' implied by the eight syllable lines:

. . .in a whole section of the second *Improvisation*, where the vocal line itself is at once syllabic and melismatic around a given note, the structure rests on the figure eight: in other words, all the important and most audible events relating to the enunciation of the verse itself have as their basis the figure eight, since the initial sonorities are eight in number. The very numerical structure of the sonnet served as a basis for the musical structure.[37]

The use of the figure eight in defining the musical structure in *Une dentelle s'abolit* can be most clearly observed in the vocal part. The first vocal line, for example, is restricted to eight pitches (Example 42). In the first two lines of the second quatrain, each of the eight syllables is presented as a semibreve marked with a pause. In the first phrase, these semibreve notes must be sung in one breath, the length of the breath defining the phrase length (Example 43).

36. Iwanka Stoianowa identifies a rather different formal movement. His analysis sees the piece in two parts, the two quatrains forming one group and the two tercets another. Stoianowa quite rightly points out that each quatrain is linked to its corresponding tercet through shared tempo markings and instrumental ensemble (Example 41). See Iwanka Stoianowa, ' "Pli selon pli". Portrait de Mallarmé', *Musique en Jeu*, xi (1973), pp 74–98.

The argument as to whether this movement should be considered as a concentric form with the quatrains and tercets gravitating around the central *très lent* section, or as a quadrilateral form with each verse balanced by an instrumental section, is an interesting one. The exact correspondence that Stoianowa identifies cannot be denied. What should be pointed out, however, is that the central *très lent* section is more than twice as long as the final one. It carries a complete melodic statement, while the final section has only melodic fragments. A consideration of the overall stress functions of the sections of the piece would reveal that the central section carries considerable weight in the musical statement, while the final one provides release. Moreover, it is entirely within Boulez's compositional doctrine that he should create a form which is not simply monovalent and capable of description in one graphic representation, but can be seen in various ways from different standpoints.

It should also be pointed out that Stoianowa's analysis refers to the original version for soprano, harp,

O	A	B	C	D	E	F	G
PAS TROP LENT	MODÉRÉ	TRÈS MOD.	TRÈS LENT	PAS TROP LENT	MODÉRÉ	PAS TROP LENT	TRÈS LENT
PARTIE VOCALE	INSTR	PARTIE VOCALE	INSTR.	PARTIE VOCALE	INSTR.	PARTIE VOCALE	INSTR
INSTRUMENTATION:							
VIBRAPHONE BLOCS MÉTAL CROTALES GONGS HARPE		VIBRAPHONE BLOCS MÉTAL CYMBALES SUSPENDUES		VIBRAPHONE BLOCS MÉTAL CROTALES CYMBALES SUSPENDUES		VIBRAPHONE BLOCS MÉTAL CROTALES GONGS	
	VIBRAPHONE HARPE		CLOCHES VIBRAPHONE TAM-TAMS CYMBALES SUSPENDUES CROTALES CAISSE CLAIRE GROSSE CAISSE HARPE		VIBRAPHONE GONGS HARPE		CLOCHES VIBRAPHONE TAM-TAMS CYMBALES SUSPENDUES CROTALES CAISSE CLAIRE GROSSE CAISSE HARPE

Example 41

vibraphone and four percussionists. However, this score is not to be performed in a complete rendition of *Pli selon pli*; it is valid only where *Le vierge, le vivace et le bel aujourd'hui* is performed on its own and in conjunction with *Improvisation II, Une dentelle s'abolit*. A detailed comparison of the fuller orchestration (soprano, two flutes doubling piccolos, clarinets in E flat and A, two alto saxophones, four horns in F, celesta, mandolin, guitar, three harps, eight percussionists, eight violas and six basses) with the original would prove a most valuable study. The formal distinctions between verse and instrumental sections are preserved in the revised version, but the contrast between them is by no means as clear. The symmetry of timbre that Stoianowa identifies is obscured and the interplay of elements in this larger ensemble has something of the continuous development which Boulez admires in Berg.

37. *C.D.*, p 95.
38. *C.D.*, p 94.

In the second phrase the line is divided by the shortest possible breath (Example 44). The third line of the second quatrain combines the technique of using eight pitches in a line with the technique of presenting each of the eight syllables as a semibreve (Example 45).

Characteristically, Boulez goes more and more deeply into the sonnets, exploring their structure in musical terms:

The sonnet is a very strict construction as far as its rhyme is concerned, and implies a particular structure for the music. For instance, for one masculine or feminine rhyme I use a certain type of structure; for another masculine or feminine rhyme I use a closely related but different structure.[38]

Here Boulez's intention is to create a contrast between the quatrains which in the sonnet form always have the same rhyme sequence: ABBA ABBA. In *Le vierge, le vivace et le bel aujourd'hui*, the A rhymes are masculine, having a stressed final syllable, and the B rhymes are feminine, the stress falling on the penultimate syllable.

U - NE DEN - - - - - - TEL - - - - - - LE S'A - - - BO - - - LIT ——

Example 42

CET U - - NA NI - - ME BLANC CON - - FLIT

Example 43

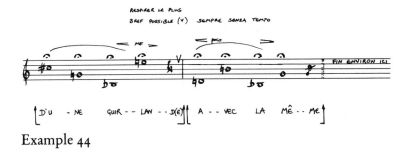

D'U - NE GUIR - - LAN - - D(E) A - - VEC LA MÊ - - ME

Example 44

EN - - - - - - - FUI CON - - TRE LA VI - - - - TRE BLÊ - - ME

Example 45

AU - JOUR - D'HUI

DES VOLS QUI N'ONT PAS   FUI

A - VEC UN COUP D'AILE IV - RE

QUE HAN-TE SOUS   LE - - GI - - VRE

Example 46

The A rhymes of the first quatrain fall on the final quaver of the bar. The B rhymes in the first quatrain have the accented and unaccented syllables set in the same way, the final syllable being set as a grace note (Example 46).

In the second quatrain, the syllables of the A rhymes are set to quicker, more complex rhythms, in phrases which rise in the first line and fall in the last. The B rhymes are also set to more complex phrases, the first contained in a rising melisma and the second as a monotone quintuplet (Example 47).

The third *Improvisation* is the only one to do justice to its title, incorporating the elements of indeterminacy developed in the previous works inspired by Mallarmé. The treatment of *À la nue*

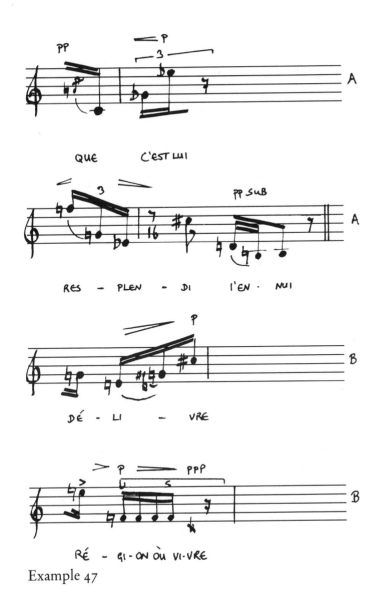

Example 47

accablante tu in a manner similar to the *Third piano sonata* was, no doubt, prompted by its similarity to *Un coup de dés*, which inspired the composition of the *Third piano sonata*. Choices must be made between different directions of melodic movement; durations are subject to different interpretations; sections may be omitted making various successions possible; and certain passages may be played with or without the vocal part (the vocal part may be omitted at the conductor's discretion, to be reintroduced at a later point prescribed by the composer).

Another important aspect of *Pli selon pli* which can be said to have its roots in Mallarmé's poetry is the conflict between direct and indirect understanding which characterises the vocal part. The use of special vocal techniques which was so prominent in *Le visage nuptial* is very restricted in *Pli selon pli*. Most of the vocal part is sung in the normal way. At the opening of *Don*, however, the voice part is marked *Parlé grave à mi-voix, éventuellement chanté*. Here Boulez uses the notational symbol for 'speech at pitch' from *Le visage nuptial* (Example 11(b)). This notation occurs again later in *Don*, where the voice sings 'pre-echoes' of following movements. Boulez asks the singer to whisper, making percussive sounds (*parlé sur le souffle comme une sorte de percussion*). The effect is reserved for monosyllables. The rest of the vocal part throughout the work is

Example 48

sung in the normal way, with the exception of the last line of *Tombeau*, which is marked *parlé sans timbre, uniquement sur le souffle*. In the third *Improvisation*, Boulez introduces quarter tones in the vocal part. Stoianowa suggests that he does this to make the music more supple and improvisational in character.[39]

Despite the severe limitation placed on the use of vocal effects, their role never becomes purely decorative. As in *Le marteau*, the contrast between speech and song has a functional purpose in defining form. Speech is reserved for the outer movements, occurring at the very beginning of the first movement and at the end of the last movement. In this way, the transition from speech to song and back to speech helps to reinforce the symmetrical plan of the work.

Possibly it was an awareness of the purity of Mallarmé's style and his concern to work within the poetic conventions that caused Boulez to eschew vocal effects. In his search for equivalents of Mallarmé's poetry, Boulez focused his attention on form, imagery and the opposition between direct and indirect understanding which is so important in symbolist poetry. The contrast between direct and indirect understanding can be seen most clearly by comparing the first and second *Improvisations*. In the first *Improvisation*, the setting is largely syllabic with only modest use of melismas. Moreover, the text is presented continuously – the music

39. Iwanka Stoianowa, ' "Pli selon pli". Portrait de Mallarmé', *Musique en Jeu*, xi (1973), p 87.

Example 49

observes the syntactic logic of the poem, clarifying the phrase and stanzaic structure. By contrast, the second *Improvisation* makes extensive use of melismas and the syllables of the text are treated as raw material to be exploited musically. The text becomes more of a succession of syllable sounds than a succession of words and phrases. As Stockhausen would put it, 'musical parameters' become dominant. This approach is justified by the theory of 'centre and absence'. Although the text is present, no effort is made to communicate its meaning directly. Boulez, of course, expects the audience to have made contact with the poetry already.[40]

Boulez's exploration of the poem from the point of view of the sonority of the words rather than their 'intelligent ordering' becomes completely clear in the start of the second quatrain, where each syllable is given a similar length and emphasis in phrases designed to be sung as slowly as possible in one breath. As Boulez puts it, the vocal line is 'at once syllabic and melismatic'[41] (Example 43). As the *Improvisation* progresses, Boulez becomes less and less concerned with 'intelligent ordering' as he separates the words of the last line of the second quatrain with pauses. Each word, no matter whether it be subject, object or verb, is treated with similar emphasis and ornamentation. Towards the end of this line, the words themselves become divided by pauses. Each syllable of the word *n'ensevelit* is treated separately. Direct understanding of the text becomes impossible here (Example 49).

The principle of 'centre and absence' can also be seen to be operating in the third *Improvisation*, which sets only the first three

40. See p 55.
41. *C.D.*, p 95.

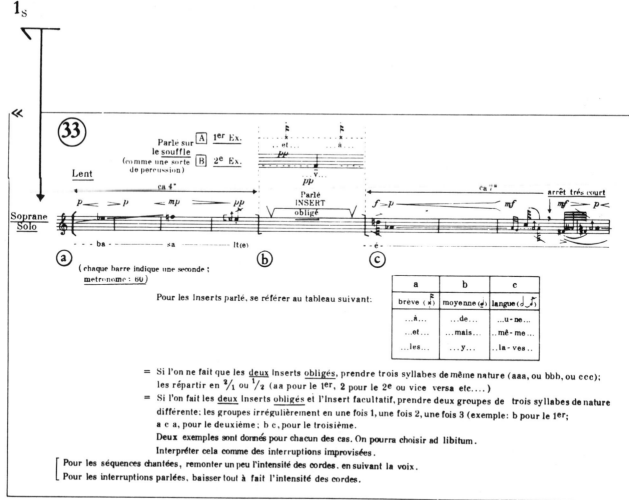

Example 50

lines of the first stanza of the sonnet. Large parts of the movement are sung in a wordless vocalise. Although the score does not specify the vowel centre to be used for this vocalise, in the recording directed by Boulez the vowel /a/ is used and this may be considered as a prolonged melisma of the first word of the first line, *À la nue accablante tu*. At this point the movement towards the domination of musical parameters is complete. The remaining text is sung in the fragmented, melismatic style of the second *Improvisation*.

The clear process of movement from coherent, syllabic speech to fragmented, melismatic singing, from the domination of lexical parameters to that of musical parameters, is easy to observe. The process is interrupted only by the pre-echoes of *Improvisations* that are heard in the first movement, *Don*. Here, too, musical parameters are dominant as fragments of the central *Improvisation*

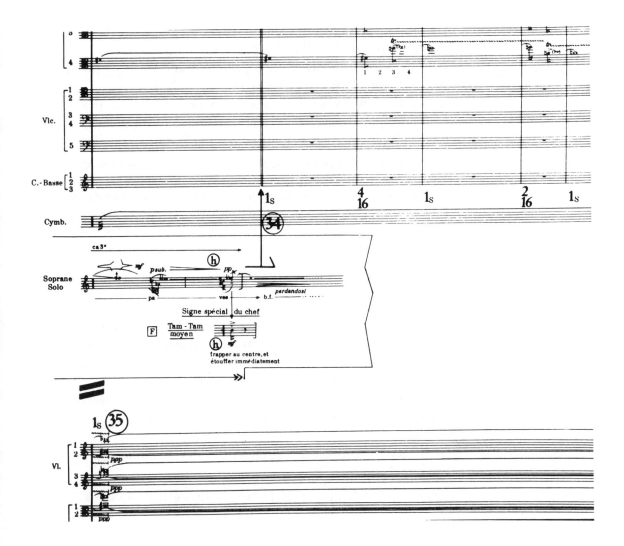

are presented completely out of context and in fragmented form (Example 50). The fragments of the *Improvisations* presented in *Don* function as pre-echoes. Like echoes, they are not exact quotations, but inexact reflections of the originals. The extracts are presented in reverse order, the pre-echo of *Improvisation III* coming first, followed by pre-echoes of *Improvisations II* and *I*.

The return to speech style in *Tombeau* is achieved only at the very end of the movement. The soprano retains a melismatic style until the last phrase. Thus, neither is the process from word to music an uninterrupted one, nor does the concentric movement from word to music and back again form a well-rounded circle. The latter would have required the most complete domination of musical parameters in the second *Improvisation* and a graded return to spoken style. Instead the work as a whole is characterised by a continuing movement towards musical domination, with an abrupt reversion to speech in the closing bars.

While one can observe clear processes and formal procedures, they are not glaringly obvious or too rigidly followed. Boulez moves close to Mallarmé's poetry in musical terms, the poetry penetrating the music on several levels. The result is not a slavish copy of Mallarmé, but a creation in his spirit:

> . . .there is a kind of total osmosis, ranging from the poetics itself to Mallarmé's choice of numerical values in his poem. I use the word 'osmosis', but there is also a complete transformation of such a profound nature that I was obliged to produce a work and a form that were entirely original. This is why I borrowed an expression from Michaux to say that at that moment the poem was both 'centre and absence' of the music.[42]

e. e. cummings: birds(here inven/

cummings ist der dichter,[43] Boulez's first setting of English poetry, was completed in its present form in 1970, but the composer's first contact with the work of cummings dates back to 1952, when his attention was drawn to the American poet by John Cage. Boulez felt an immediate attraction to cummings's poetry but delayed any attempt to set it until he felt a greater competency with the English language.

Characteristically, what attracted Boulez to cummings was his 'work on language':

> . . .cummings goes further than Mallarmé: Mallarmé arranged his words in a new way and tried to find syntactical ways of combining them, but cummings enters into the vocabulary itself. . .[44]

Boulez was perfectly aware that cummings, in some respects, is a Romantic and not a Modernist poet, much of his poetry being taken up with subjects of love and nature, and his involvement with his subjects certainly not achieving the coolness and remove that characterises much Modern poetry. Nor can cummings boast Mallarmé's complexity of syntax and imagery:

> He [cummings] *is* less complex. . .He does not go further into the poetic universe. . .the poems of cummings, when compared with a poem like *Un coup de dés*, for instance, are relatively simple.[45]

Boulez's concern with the poetry of cummings, like his concern with Mallarmé, was to make a musical transposition of his poetic innovations:

> . . .[cummings] makes marvellous use of double meanings, and of ambiguities between words. He also uses the parenthesis with quite superb mastery. You may say that it seems difficult to use parentheses in music, since they cannot be heard, but what interests me is not to transcribe cummings's discoveries literally into music, but to find a transcription of his world in my own.[46]

42. Ibid.
43. Boulez explains the rather surprising fact that his first setting of English poetry should carry a German title in the following way:
> I could not find a title for the work. It was due for performance, first at Ulm then at Stuttgart, and I was asked for the title so that the programmes could be printed well in advance. In a letter in German – and as far as I can remember, my German was probably not very good – I wrote 'I have not yet found a title for the work but all that I can tell you now is that cummings is the poet I have chosen'. I then got a reply from a secretary who had obviously misunderstood my letter: 'As for your work "cummings is the poet. . ." ', in German, ' "cummings ist der dichter. . ." '. I felt there could not possibly be a better title than that, which had come about completely by accident. [*C.D.*, p 98.]
44. *C.D.*, p 97.
45. Ibid.
46. Ibid.

birds(here inven/ is taken from cummings's collection of 1935, entitled *No thanks*. In many respects, it is typical of cummings's work. There is an obvious concern with typographic layout: fragmentation of the vocabulary creates ambiguities within words, and there is an intriguing use of parentheses.

One of cummings's many natural descriptions, the poem describes the song and flight of birds at twilight. The symbol of flight is one honoured by poetic tradition and the use of this symbol links the poetry of *cummings ist der dichter* with the poetry of *Pli selon pli*. The passing birds evoke the changing of seasons and the layout of the poem may well be intended as a typographical mimesis of migrating birds. That Boulez feels the poetry describes the coming of spring is suggested by his subtitle for the work, *First birds*. cummings's natural descriptions are almost invariably connected with expressions of love, but Norman Friedman suggests that the most important meaning of the bird symbol in cummings's poetry is as a symbol of life's truth.[47] He quotes cummings's *until and i heard* in support of his theory:

until and i heard
a certain a bird
i dreamed i could sing
but like nothing
           are the joys
of his voice[48]

For cummings, the world is 'real' or 'unreal'; 'unreal' when it is caught in the 'conspiracy of clocks and calendars', and 'real' when it transcends day-to-day reality. *birds(here inven/* is a call to 'real' life:

    Be)look
now
    (come
soul;

Thus, cummings's poem describes poetic flight, the coming of spring, an expression of love, an audition of life's truth and a call to 'reality'.

> birds(
>   here,inven
> ting air
> U
>)sing
>
> tw
> iligH(
> t's
>   v
>   va
>   vas(
> vast

47. Norman Friedman, *e.e. cummings: the art of his poetry*, London, 1968.
48. e.e. cummings, *Complete poems*, vol. ii, London, 1968.

```
                               ness.Be)look
          now
                 (come
          soul;
          &:and

          who
                 s)e
                        voi
          c
          es
          (
             are
                   ar
                      a
```

Clearly, typography plays a very important part in cummings's poetic expression. Boulez's attempt to find equivalents for cummings's typography extended his work on the *Piano sonata no. 3*, which sought equivalents for the typography of Mallarmé's *Un coup de dés*. The typography of *birds(here inven/* has as its basic means an interplay of print and page, the foreground words and punctuation, and the background page. Boulez makes from this duality two opposing morphological components.[49] He creates a contrast between sustained sound (representing the background) and short fragmentary interjections of sound (representing the foreground). These components are combined in three ways. They may be superimposed so that continuous sound provided by one group becomes the 'background' for interjections of 'foreground' of another. They may be combined in what Stoianowa describes as 'successive opposition': here, the components are isolated from each other and contrasted successively. A third technique combines the technique of superimposition and successive opposition in a polymorphic manipulation. This is a multiple procedure in which the origin of the morphological components may no longer be recognisable. 'Foreground' interjections may be combined with 'background' elements in such a way that the difference between the two components cannot directly be discerned. However, the morphological division continues to be generative in the compositional process.

Boulez treats these three techniques of manipulating the morphological components in three different sections. It is perhaps surprising to find that the piece opens, not with a presentation of the components in their most recognisable form – the superimposition of components – but with the polymorphic section. This section is in two parts, the first being for orchestra and female voices (pp 1–5 of the published score), the second for orchestra and male voices

49. The derivation of morphological components was identified by Iwanka Stoianowa in 'Verbe et son "centre absence" sur *cummings ist der dichter*...de Boulez, *O King* de Berio et *Für Stimmen...Missa est* de Schnebel', *Musique en Jeu*, xvi (1974), 79–102.

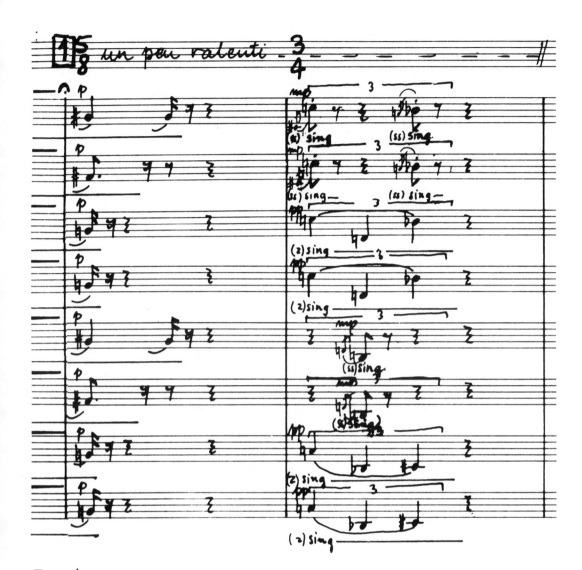

Example 51

(pp 6–13). An unusual feature of this setting is the opposition of
male and female voices who never sing together. In fact, female
voices are heard only in this opening passage. The second section
treats the elements in successive opposition (pp 14–19). Here voices
and orchestra work together, neither being particularly associated
with one or other morphological component. Finally, we arrive at
the section that superimposes the elements (pp 20–26). Here voices
and strings create a sound continuum as a background to
instrumental solos. However, there is not a simple dualism, the
strings and voices often interrupting their own continuum with
dynamic swells and tremolos which, themselves, constitute inter-

Example 52

jections. Boulez appears to have reversed the traditional procedure of exposition and development. In *cummings ist der dichter*, development precedes exposition. In this respect, the work is innovative.

Boulez's musical transcription of cummings's poem is by no means restricted to this typographical derivation of morphological components, his concern being to find equivalents for all aspects of the poem. He takes up cummings's word play. The ambiguities the poet creates within words are identified by Boulez and exploited in the composition. For example, the word 'using' is divided into two parts, 'U/sing/', creating two meanings. The first is its more logical meaning in its context 'birds here using twilight's vastness', the second, 'you sing'. Boulez shows his awareness of this ambiguity by using the phonetic symbol (z) and (s) to differentiate the two meanings: (z) is the voiced sibilant from 'using' and (s) the unvoiced sibilant from 'you sing' (Example 51).

Boulez also picks up the parallels between words or phonemes

Example 53

suggested by the text. The typographical highlighting and parallelism of 'ting' (from 'inventing') and 'sing' (from 'using') is brought
out in the setting (Example 52). Similarly, Boulez brings together
'ds' (from 'birds') and 't's' (from 'twilight's') (Example 53). The
phonetic fragmentation in Boulez's setting is not the result of
compositional whim but something that is clearly suggested by the
poem.

cummings's poetry, fragmented and punctuated as it is, must
always be 're-created' by the reader. The reader must reassemble the
phonemes into words and the words into lines. This means that he
will return and reread word groups, often finding different meanings and parallels in the text. Boulez seeks a musical equivalent for
this, too. His setting repeatedly doubles back on word groups,
discovering different phonetic and semantic combinations. The
setting is not, however, capricious. Boulez continues to pay attention to the 'intelligent ordering' of the text. Despite the many
repetitions and doublings back, the text is preserved in its original

order as a *fil conducteur*. Although a word may be repeated many times after its first appearance, it will, generally, not be heard until the text which precedes it has been presented. The *fil conducteur* slightly rearranges the text order so that the sequence 'be look now come soul and' becomes 'now be look soul and come', which actually makes the meaning slightly more immediate. It is import-

Example 54

ant to note that Boulez's setting ends here. He does not set the last words:

```
who
    s)e
       voi
c
es
(
are
   ar
     a
```

What may appear to be a haphazard manipulation of words and phonemes is usually carefully organised and logically thought out. Words which, at first glance, seem to be spread over the page in an indiscriminate manner are often placed according to some principle of text-aggregation. For example, the basses and tenors in Example 54 use the words and phonemes: *birds*; *in*; *here*; *air*; *sing*; *ven*; *ting*; *twi*; *ligh*; *t's*; *vast*. The words and phonemes are aggregated in such a way that the successive entries create the phrase 'birds here

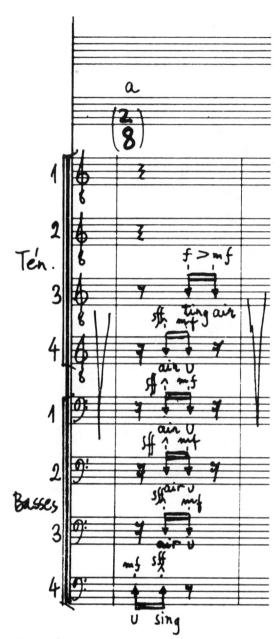

Example 55

Example 56

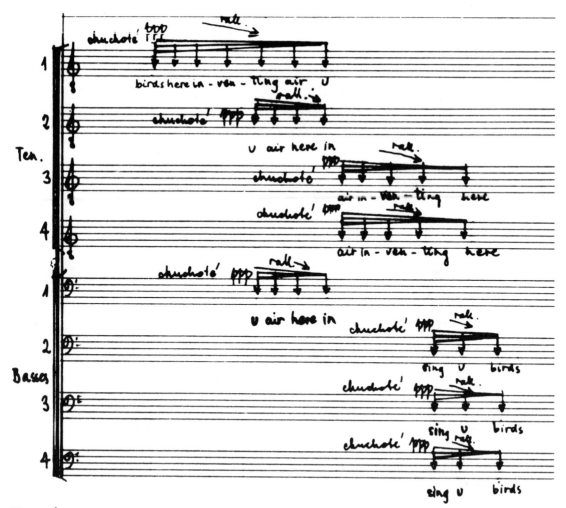

Example 57

inventing air using twilight's vast', the first phrase of the poem in its
original sequence. Within this logical aggregation word-play does
occur. Reading horizontally, we find: *air sing*; *ting sing*; *in sing*;
here sing; *birds sing*; which realise the word-play suggested by
cummings's poem. Boulez here achieves a conjunction of logical
ordering and word-play. Vertical groups observe similarly logical
aggregations. In Example 55, the words are aggregated *up* through
the group; in Example 56 they are aggregated *down* the group.

The range of vocal techniques is limited in *cummings ist der
dichter*. Most of the music is sung in the conventional way. There is,
however, recourse to unpitched (or, more accurately, pitch-inde-

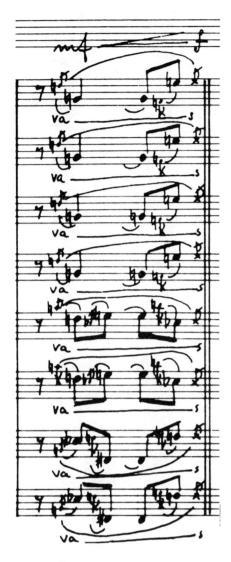

Example 58

terminate) whispering, notated by triangular note-heads on the
central line of the stave (Example 57). Triangular note-heads are
also used for pitch-indeterminate phonetic sounds (Example 53). A
cross note-head is used for phonetic sounds at the end of words.
These are notated as specific pitches, usually an extension of the
sung pitch that precedes them. However, they are inevitably sounds
without determined pitch (Example 58). In the last bar, Boulez calls
for the voices to produce 'head tones'. Although modification of
vocal techniques is not a primary form-giving factor, as it was in *Le
visage nuptial*, certain vestiges of this function remain. For example,
the change from female to male voices in the first section is

Example 59

reinforced by a change in vocal emission, male voices entering with whispered tones, following the exclusively sung passages for female voices.

Melisma is used in great profusion. Boulez clearly expects the 'subtler effort'[50] of his listeners as he treats the text as 'centre and absence'. Initially, the setting observes fairly conventional proportions of musical and semantic parameters (Example 59) but, as the piece progresses, phonetic fragmentation becomes more frequent and melismas become larger (Examples 60, 61). The movement from relative textual clarity to fragmentation and melismatic extension observes a more conventional process of development, which counters the inverse development of morphological components.

cummings's poetry made a refreshing change from the terse and complex poetry of Mallarmé. Boulez comments that cummings's poetry helped him rediscover 'a certain freshness',[51] a freshness that characterised the earlier work, *Le soleil des eaux*. It seems that Boulez reserves a style for nature topics which features lush sonorities and a more moderate harmonic and intervallic vocabulary. Indeed, *cummings ist der dichter* is lushly scored. It calls for a wind group consisting of flute, two oboes, two cors anglais and

50. 'The subtler effort I am now proposing implies that knowledge of the poem has already been acquired'; Pierre Boulez, 'Son et verbe', *R.A.*, p. 60.
51. *C.D.*, p 97.

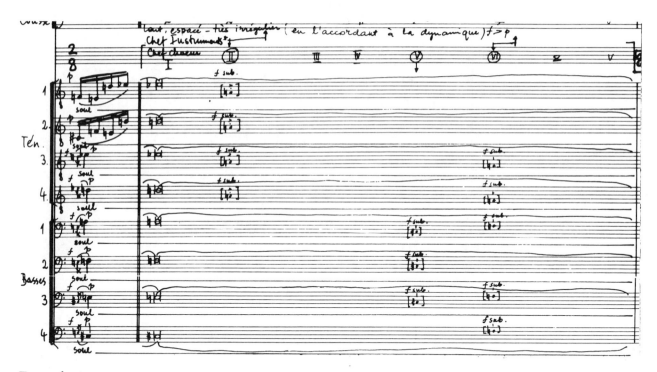

Example 60

bassoon; a brass group of two trumpets, three horns and trombone; a group of three harps; a string group of violin, three violas, three 'cellos and bass; and a chorus of four sopranos, four altos, four tenors and four basses. The groups are often treated as individual layers of sonority in a 'contrapuntal' style, in which each group constitutes one voice (Example 61).

Paul Griffiths has been rather dismissive of *cummings ist der dichter*. He feels that it represents an 'uncertainty of direction'.[52] Although *cummings ist der dichter* does in some respects constitute a reversion to the sound world of *Le soleil des eaux*, it is, in every

52. Paul Griffiths, *Boulez*, p 57.

Example 61

* à l'intérieur d'un ou deux chiffres romains
a) trémolo, b) trémolo < >, c) trémolo > <

other respect, a logical extension of his ideas of the use of poetry in composition. It continues the search for musical equivalents to literature, it treats the text as 'centre and absence', and it allows the poem to become an irrigation of the composition. Boulez has surely succeeded in his stated objective: 'not to transcribe cummings's discoveries literally into music, but to find a transcription of his world. . .'[53]

53. *C.D.*, p 97.

V · A Polyphony of Styles

I understand what Boulez is saying. . .and it's true. . .He's
become a unique thing in the world. But this uniqueness
by exclusion is a very special kind of quality. You can
always identify this 'style'. A vaster mind, however, tries
to create a polyphony of styles. . .[1]

Stockhausen, 1971

Certainly Boulez has developed a very individual approach and
occupies a unique position. A part of this individuality results from
his admission of extramusical disciplines into the compositional
process – his reaction to the literary medium being the most striking
example of this. But how does his use of texts compare with his
contemporaries' approach? In this chapter, consideration is given to
other composers' techniques of relating sound and word. Of
course, it will not be possible to provide a fully comprehensive
account of contemporary practice, but the various techniques of
treating texts can be described and certain comparisons can be
made.

Since 1945, a multiplicity of techniques of text-setting have
developed. The interaction of the musical and literary media is
many-faceted, the composer making decisions and choices in the
following key areas:

1 The selection of text(s)
2 The style(s) of vocal production
3 Text intelligibility
4 The relationship of musical and textual form
5 The affective relationship of music and text.

In each category, choices are made from a spectrum of possibilities.
In the following analysis, each spectrum is described in terms of the
cardinal points which determine it. However, composers will often
draw on the subtler shades which connect these points.

1 *The selection of texts (spectrum: poetic text ⟷ paralinguistic text)*

Before a composer can commence a text-setting, he must choose the

1. Karlheinz Stockhausen in *Conversations with the composer*, ed. Jonathan Cott, London, 1974, p 104.

text or texts on which he is going to work. A great many different types of text are available to him and his selection of text or texts constitutes his first compositional decision – before he can set one word to music, he must compose with language itself. The composer will choose from the following text-types:

(i)   Poetic texts
    (a)   a single poem
    (b)   all or some of the poems of a work
    (c)   poems of one author from different collections
    (d)   poems by different authors

(ii)   Non-poetic texts
    (a)   found texts (prose passages from any source)
    (b)   catalogue texts (successions of words having little or no semantic continuity)

(iii) Paralinguistic texts ('texts' consisting of phonetics and behavioural sounds – laughing, crying, grunting, etc. having no lexical or semantic content).[2]

All of Boulez's settings fall in the first category: they are all poetic texts. His three Char settings, *Le visage nuptial*, *Le soleil des eaux*, and *Le marteau sans maître*, belong to category (i)(b), basing musical works on combinations of poems from a single collection. *Pli selon pli* falls in category (i)(c), as it combines Mallarmé's texts, belonging to different periods of the poet's life. *cummings ist der dichter* falls in category (i)(a), being the setting of a single poem. Boulez spurns the other text sources. His choice is restricted exclusively to poetic texts. Furthermore, he does not venture to combine poetic texts by more than one author.

Examples of composers' use of text types not exploited by Boulez abound. Hans Werner Henze (b. 1926) combines poems by Ho Chi Minh, Bertolt Brecht, Giuseppe Ungaretti and many others in his politically motivated collection of songs entitled *Stimmen*. *Laborintus II*, by Luciano Berio (b. 1925), illustrates the use of non-poetic texts. This large-scale dramatic work for reciter, singers, orchestra and tape uses a text prepared by the poet Edoardo Sanguineti. It consists of quotations from Dante's *La vita nuova*, *La Divina Commedia*, and *Il convivio*, and catalogue-texts evoking 'All, all, all from the candy to the honey, from the Sino–Indian frontier war to the idola tribus, to Brussels, to Paris, to my feet, to the answering service. . .'. One of the few pieces to use an exclusively paralinguistic text is *Aventures* by György Ligeti (b. 1923) (Example 62). More commonly, pieces use paralinguistic elements in combination with conventional texts, as does Berio's

2. Such texts do not exist before the composition but are generated and grow as the composition develops.

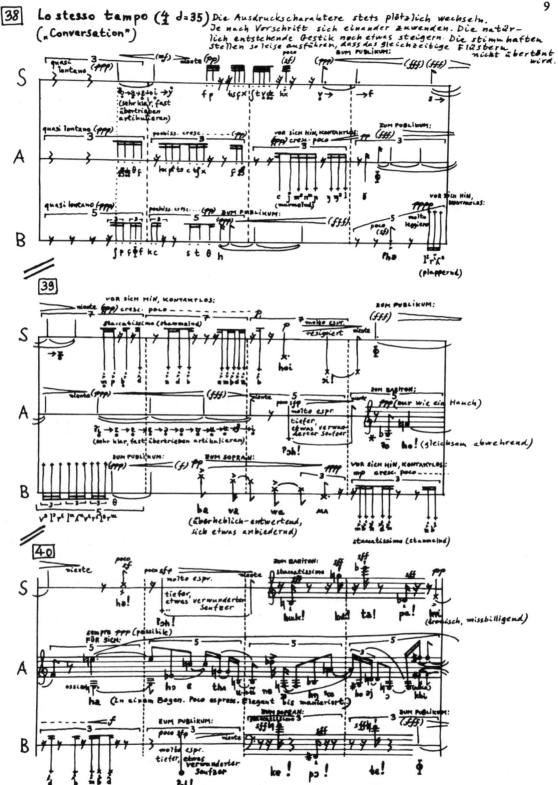

Example 62

Sequenza III for solo female voice, which interpolates behavioural sounds into the setting of Markus Kutter's poem (Example 63).

2 *Techniques of vocal production (spectrum: speech ⟷ music)*

The speech–music spectrum permits a multitude of gradations, in which the components of speech and music may be present in different proportions. The following represent the cardinal points of the spectrum:

(i)   Recitation
      (a)   unnotated
      (b)   with notated rhythms
      (c)   with notated rhythms and relative pitch indication (e.g. notation around a central line denoting middle register).

(ii)   *Sprechgesang*

(iii)   Conventional singing
      (a)   with dominant linguistic parameters (syllabic)
      (b)   with dominant musical parameters (melismatic)[3]

(iv)   Phonetic extraction

(v)   Production of non-lexical sounds
      (a)   paralinguistic sounds
      (b)   voice as a musical instrument.

Boulez has explored only the central ground of this spectrum. He has never allowed the freedom of unnotated recitation and he has never had call to introduce non-lexical sounds. However, his exploration of the first four categories (with the exception of unnotated recitation) has been most systematic. His first two Char settings constitute a thorough examination of the gradations available between notated recitation and conventional singing. *Pli selon pli* uses phonetic extraction for the first time, although the work is still largely dominated by conventional singing. Some notated recitation is used here, so that the work spans the spectrum from notated recitation to phonetic extraction. *cummings ist der dichter* belongs largely to the third and fourth categories, combining conventional singing and phonetic extraction and, like *Pli selon pli*, its use of notated recitation is restricted. Boulez's vocal works have thus progressed through the spectrum from speech to music, the early detailed analysis of notated recitation and *Sprechgesang* forms giving way to a more broadly based combination of the available styles. With conventional singing as the central point, and

3. Conventional singing implies the combination of music and speech in specific proportions, in a usage which has developed over the years and has reached the status of a musical convention. Within this convention, however, the composer may move towards the parameters of speech or music.

Example 63

other effects reserved to add colour, Boulez has developed a sophisticated and balanced palette of vocal styles.

Although few composers have explored the gradations between recitation and conventional singing as systematically as Boulez, there has been no lack of investigation of the styles. Berio is as comprehensive in his usage as Boulez is systematic. The opening of *Laborintus II* combines the extremes of phonetic extraction and recitation (Example 64). Here, Berio extends Boulez's usage by employing *unnotated* recitation. He gives his reciter a freedom which Boulez would never allow – he allows the text to be itself, rhythm and pitch being determined by the text and the reciter's understanding of it.[4] The work goes on to exploit many of the available possibilities of the spectrum: recitation with notated rhythms; recitation with notated rhythms and relative pitch; and conventional singing. Moreover, Berio extends the styles of vocal production beyond the speech–music spectrum. He modifies the vocal tone, asking for unvoiced passages,[5] and passages with a 'rasping throat sound'. Berio displays a sophisticated knowledge of the detail of vocal production and his notation exhibits a great attention to detail. In Example 65, from *Circles* (1960), he tells the

4. In the recording of *Laborintus II*, the recitation is handled most expertly by the poet Edoardo Sanguineti. Berio is a composer who responds to collaborators. It is doubtful whether his remarkable innovations in the vocal field could have taken place without the close cooperation of his former wife, the singer, Cathy Berberian. Similarly, Berio can leave passages of recitation unnotated, knowing that they can be delivered for him in expert fashion by Sanguineti.

5. This is not, of course, unique to Berio. Boulez also calls for whispering in *cummings ist der dichter*.

to susan and marina

laborintus II

per voci, strumenti e registrazioni (1965)
testo di edoardo sanguineti

luciano berio
(1925)

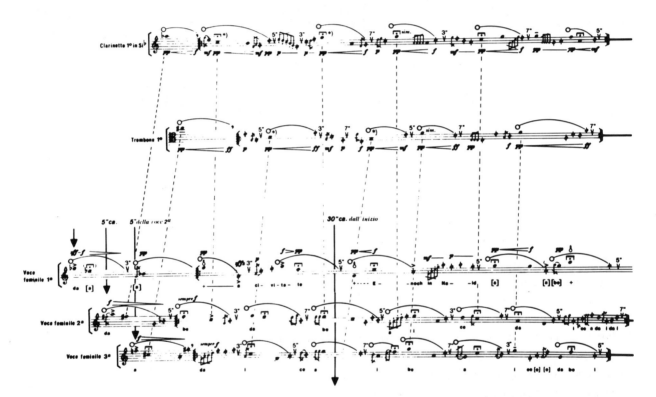

Testo: In quella parte; in quella parte della mia memoria; in quella parte del libro; in quella parte del libro della mia memoria incipit vita nova: e apparve vestita di nobilissimo colore, umile e onesto, sanguigno: ecce Deus, ecce Deus fortior me: dominabitur mihi.

In that part, in that part of my memory, in that part of the book, in that part of the book of my memory incipit vita nova. She appeared dressed in noble colours, modest, pure, and sanguine: Ecce Deus fortior me: dominabitur mihi.

*) Imitando e continuando lo stesso suono della voce feminile
  Imitating and continuing the sound of the voice

Universal Edition No. 13992 M

Example 64

Example 65

Example 66

singer exactly when to make the transition from vowel to consonant in a melismatic phrase. This movement between melisma and *bouche fermée* singing has become something of a hallmark of the composer and fairly common usage in avant-garde composers (Example 66, from Harrison Birtwistle's *Cantata*, 1971). Equally characteristic of Berio's vocal style is his use of non-lexical sounds. *Sequenza III* constitutes one of his most extensive explorations of paralinguistic and instrumental properties of the voice. In it, we hear (and see) everything from a dental tremolo and whispering to coughing and bursts of laughter. Tongue clicks and modification of the vocal tone by covering the mouth with the hand can be regarded as 'instrumental' modifications.

Of course, Berio has not been the only composer to explore the large reservoir of vocal techniques. There seems to be no limit to composers' invention in this field. Nothing is taboo – everything goes, from eroticism (Berio's *Visage*, 1961) to the fully fledged scream (Maxwell Davies's *Revelation and Fall*, 1966).

A less theatrical branch of exploration of vocal styles and techniques also exists. Recently, interest has developed in the ability of the human voice to produce harmonics.[6] Harmonics are produced by the use of vowel centres and a vocal technique which causes the

6. Although this is a fairly recent development in Western music, it has been a part of music-making in certain Oriental regions for some time. The Mongolian technique of ululating is a well developed technique of harmonic production.

defining vowel formant to become clearly audible above the fundamental.[7] Because the production of harmonics is connected with the formation of vowel centres, it may be combined with phonetic extraction, as it is in Stockhausen's *Stimmung* (1968). Alternatively, it may be used without any lexical reference, the listener's attention being directed to the sound of the harmonic and not to its source – the vowel centre. In *Pneuma* (1976) and *Chanson de jeste* (1978), Denis Smalley has developed techniques of harmonic production using a stream of air directed against the palate or an unvoiced throat sound. With such techniques, the vocal organs may be used to produce sounds which are primarily musical and have little or no reference to text, lexical or paralinguistic.

3 *Text intelligibility (spectrum: direct intelligibility ⟷ centre and absence)*

The cardinal points of the spectrum of text intelligibility are two in number:

(i)   Direct intelligibility
(ii)   Centre and absence.

Intelligibility is dependent on the style of vocal production employed and the audibility of the speaking or singing voices. A voice may be speaking in normal speech style but, if this voice is 'masked' by other sounds, the text will not be intelligible and the setting will approach the category of centre and absence.

As we have seen, much of Boulez's vocal work has been preoccupied with movement within this spectrum. But Boulez is not the only composer to have exploited this device. Berio's vocal music plays with intelligibility in a most remarkable way using a multitude of techniques, including masking, polylingualism, and simultaneous text presentation. Stockhausen's *Gesang der Jünglinge* has a very individual and systematic approach to the question of text intelligibility. Stockhausen blends sung notes (the voice of a boy treble) with electronically produced ones (sine waves) to create a sound-continuum:

The intention, therefore, is, by selecting individual steps from a sound–word continuum, to let 'speech' proceed from the composition. . .it is possible to have a continuous transition from listening to comprehension. It can be said that the more the sound-aspect dominates in a structure the more typical of music it is; the more the word–motive aspect dominates (sound-connections with fixed meaning), the more typical of speech it is; and speech can approach music, music can approach speech up to the point of the dissolution of the boundaries of sound and meaning.[8]

7. The tone quality of a musical instrument is, in part, defined by the predominance of certain partials in the harmonic series. These secondary sounds or overtones condition our perception of timbre. Our ability to understand language is dependent on the perception of timbre, for vowels are not distinguished in fundamental pitch but by their partials or formants. The production of vocal harmonics is equivalent to the production of instrumental harmonics, although the means of production is different.

8. Karlheinz Stockhausen, op cit, p 49.

This procedure is justified by the theory of centre and absence:

Jünglinge reminds us of general knowledge: if the word 'preiset' (praise) occurs at one moment and the word 'Herrn' (Lord) at another – or vice versa – the listener is reminded of a word-connection he has always known: the words are memorised. . .and the details of the content are of secondary importance, the concentration is directed upon the sacredness. . .[9]

4 *Formal interaction (spectrum: imitation of textual form ⟷ ignorance of textual form)*

In considering formal interaction of text and music, it is necessary to divide the classification into two parts, to consider poetic texts and non-poetic texts independently. The poem, as a fully adapted artistic medium, carries a consciously composed form, while non-poetic texts, particularly catalogue texts, have less clearly defined form:

(i)　　Poetic texts
　　　(a)　Imitation of poetic form
　　　(b)　Superimposition of musical and poetic form
　　　(c)　Ignorance of poetic form

(ii)　　Non-poetic texts
　　　(a)　Imitation of textual form
　　　(b)　Superimposition of musical and textual form
　　　(c)　Ignorance of textual form.

The music of Boulez's first two Char settings maintains a close imitative relationship with the text. In *Le marteau sans maître*, however, Boulez began to explore the possibilities of superimposing a musical form over a poetic form. This tendency became pronounced in *Pli selon pli*, where Boulez sought consciously 'to choose very strict forms from Mallarmé in order to graft on to them a proliferation of music sprouting from an equally strict form. . .'[10] In *cummings ist der dichter*, the formal imitation takes place indirectly, the typographical form of the poem generating morphological components which are then arranged in three separate sections. The formal relationship of text and music in this work is substantially more sophisticated than in Boulez's early settings. It approaches the category of superimposition of musical and poetic form, but this is achieved through what is essentially a process of imitation.

Imitation of poetic or textual form is far more common than ignorance of it. Berio's *Sequenza III* for solo female voice, despite its excursion into paralinguistics and theatre, still adheres to the form of the chosen text – a poem by Markus Kutter. The poem is arranged in the form of a matrix containing nine phrases which can

9. Ibid, p 58.
10. *C.D.*, p 94.

be read down, across or diagonally. A conventional reading (from left to right, across and down) renders the greatest semantic continuity. However, the typographical form contradicts this continuity and the reader is made to look for different sequences in the text. Berio's setting explores both the semantic continuity and the 'word-play' of the poem.

give me	a few words	for a woman
to sing	a truth	allowing us
to build a house	without worrying	before night comes

The first phrase of the setting combines syllables from different parts of the text, the syllables to be reiterated in any order:

to	from 'to sing' or 'to build'
/co/	from 'before night comes'
us	from 'allowing us'
for	from 'before night comes'
be	from 'before night comes'.

Although the score is replete with this sort of phonetic fragmentation, the semantic continuity, the *fil conducteur*, is present and highlighted, being set to specific pitches, amid the profusion of paralinguistic sounds.

For a composer to ignore completely the formal implications of his chosen text is most uncommon. Stockhausen argues, in his article 'Music and Speech', that Luigi Nono's *Il canto sospeso* applies an alienation technique to its texts, which consist of the letters of political prisoners condemned to death.

When setting certain parts of the letters about which one should be particularly ashamed that they had been written, the musician assumes the attitude only of the composer who had previously selected the letters: he does not interpret, he does not comment. He rather reduces speech to its sounds and makes music with them. . .The texts are not delivered, but rather concealed in. . .regardlessly strict and dense musical form. . .[11]

However, Nono has rejected Stockhausen's assertion, claiming that any text suppression observed by Stockhausen is coincidental and not intended by him.[12] Although a composer may move some distance from the form of the text he is setting, it is very rare for him to achieve the extreme of the above spectrum – a complete ignorance of the text's formal implications.

5 Affective relationship (spectrum: imitation of textual mood ⟷ ignorance of textual mood)

Broadly speaking, the composer may imitate the textual mood, may establish an affective relationship, in one of two ways:

11. Karlheinz Stockhausen, op. cit, p 49.
12. Ibid.

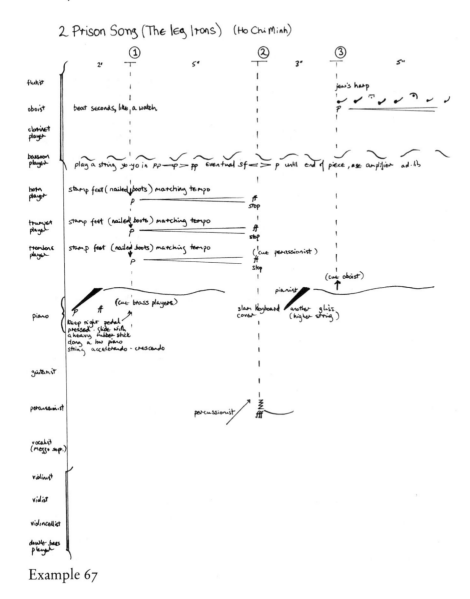

Example 67

(i)   Direct imitation
      (a)   on a low architectonic level (word-painting)
      (b)   on a high architectonic level (overall mood).

Otherwise, the composer may choose to oppose music and text:

(ii)   Ignorance of textual mood

   All of Boulez's settings are related to the text, according to the principles of mimesis. But he eschews the extremes to which other composers are prepared to go – for example, Henze's setting of Ho Chi Minh's *Prison song* creates a mimesis that borders on theatrical

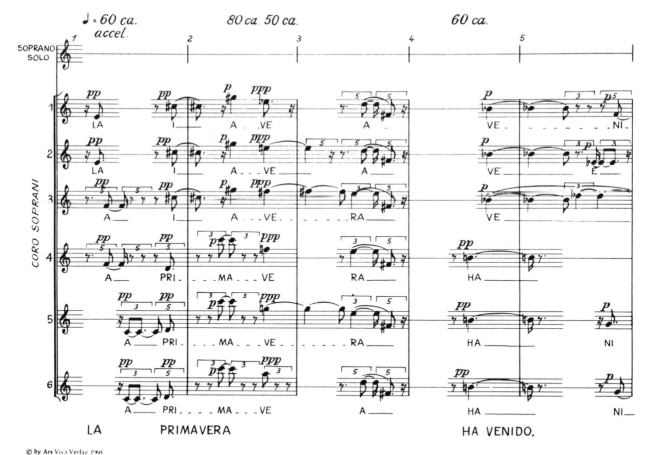

Example 68

representation (Example 67). Nono's cool treatment of the war prisoners' texts in *Il canto sospeso* has already been noted. Note, also, Nono's treatment of the words *La primavera ha venido* (Spring has come) in *'Ha venido' canciones para Silvia* (Example 68).

Music–theatre

All of Boulez's vocal works are designed to be presented according to the conventions of the Western concert. His decision to 'remain outside the theatre'[13] focuses the attention of the audience uniquely on the musical composition. None of his vocal works has sought to exploit the dramatic potential of the concert environment. It is ironic that Boulez found inspiration for the development of varied vocal techniques in Schoenberg's *Pierrot lunaire* but managed totally to ignore the dramatic implications of the piece; for this monodrama, with a small group of instrumentalists, has become the model for many dramatic works which, avoiding the conventions of

13. Pierre Boulez, 'Son et verbe', *R.A.*, p 58.

both opera and the recital, create a new medium in which a performer's dramatic presence can be realised.

The degree of theatricality introduced into works of music–theatre varies enormously. In Berio's *Circles*, for example, the singer moves in a semi-circular motion between three stands while the percussionists perform in circles of instruments. In *Sequenza III*, the dramatic component is more substantial and the fusion between dramatic and musical components more complete. *Laborintus II* defies classification: Berio describes it as 'a theatrical event, an allegory, a documentary, a pantomime, etc. It may be performed in the theatre, in concert, on television, on the radio, in the open air, etc.'[14] In all of these works, Berio extends the intermedial interaction beyond the dualistic music–literature confrontation into a three-way fusion of music, literature and drama. In this way, Berio has explored a dimension totally ignored by Boulez.

Other composers have gone still further in the attempt to create a music–drama fusion. It is a very long way from *Le visage nuptial* to Bussotti's *La passion selon Sade* (1966) which 'turns chamber music into semi-opera',[15] or Stockhausen's *Originale* (1960) in which 'the dramatic impulse is created. . .by the situations suggested by the various types of recording media, the tape recorder, the canvas, . . .the newspaper, and their attendant operators.'[16] Perhaps the most extensive exploration in the field of instrumental theatre, or dramatised music, has been carried out by Kagel, who has offered us musico–dramatic spectacles, from a sporting confrontation for two cellists and percussion in *Match* (1964), to a choreographed promenade for five performers with walking sticks in *Pas de cinq* (1965); from a musical performance on household tools in *Unter Strom* (1969), to the anti-opera *Staatstheater* (1967–70). Boulez remains among the 'few of Kagel's contemporaries. . .who have remained uninfluenced by the constant fecundity of his invention'.[17] Boulez has roundly dismissed the neo-dada and the happening:

Musicians have always been in the rearguard of the revolutions of others; in music Dadaism still retains the prestige (and naivety) which it has long since lost everywhere else; its flimsy veils hide the sweet sickness of rosy dilettantism. We have learnt from Nietzsche that God is dead, then from Dadaism that Art is dead; there is no longer any need to return to the flood, and to do a reckless revision course on the brilliant demonstrations of yesteryear.[18]

Electro–acoustic music and the voice

Electro–acoustic music is a realm of compositional activity of which Boulez is by no means ignorant. Between 1951 and 1952, he made two short but important tape compositions: *Étude sur un son* (Study on one sound) and *Étude sur sept sons* (Study on seven

14. Luciano Berio's introductory comments to the score *Laborintus II*, Universal Edition, Milan, 1976.
15. Reginald Smith Brindle, *The new music*, London, 1975, pp 149–52.
16. Robin Maconie, *The works of Karlheinz Stockhausen*, London, 1976, p 153.
17. Josef Häusler's article on Kagel in *The New Grove dictionary of music and musicians*.
18. Pierre Boulez, *O.M.T.*, p 24.

sounds), both for single track tape. In 1958, he made his first essay in the mixed genre, combining five-track tape and orchestra in *Poésie pour pouvoir*. Today, Boulez is involved in the live electronic transformation of sounds of conventional instruments in his realisation of *...explosante-fixe...* (1971).[19] But he has been highly critical of concerts of tape music, describing them as 'crematorium ceremonies'.[20] *Poésie pour pouvoir* was abandoned after its first performance and it remains to be seen whether it will emerge in revised form.

Other composers have been less inhibited by the tape medium. The past twenty-five years have seen the most remarkable developments in what constitutes the newest compositional tool. The rapid development of electronic and electro-acoustic technology, from the early studios to computer synthesis, is without parallel in contemporary music. Perhaps only the rapid development of new vocal techniques can begin to match its swift progress. Moreover, it has been argued that the development of studio techniques has influenced the development of vocal techniques; that these are interrelated developments.[21]

Tape composition allows an analytical approach to the voice. Vocal sounds can be closely analysed in the studio, broken down and made to perform in a manner humanly impossible. Compositionally, what results is a style in which phonetic components are made to observe new criteria. Stockhausen's *Gesang der Jünglinge* (1955–56) was undoubtedly the first important work in this field. *Gesang* is a conscious attempt to make a continuum of speech and music, to make electronic sounds approximate to the sound images of language and to take language to the point of pure sound. Berio's objectives in *Thema (Omaggio a Joyce)* (1958) were very similar to Stockhausen's in *Gesang*. Berio's aim was to create a 'complete continuity and perfect integration, so that it will be possible to achieve a new kind of relationship between word and sound, poetry and music'.[22] With the development of the studio, it became possible for language to be worked in a new way, 'intensifying and increasing the transformation of vocal colours..."decomposing" the words and reordering the resultant vocal material...'[23]

Tape may be used in works of mixed genre combining live vocal performance with recorded sound. Nono's work in this medium is political rather than analytical. *La fabbrica illuminata* (1964) provides its solo soprano with a background of factory noise and treated choral singing. *Y entoces comprendió* (1969–70) combines live singers, actors, choir and tape. The tape includes phonetic extractions of the text, quotations from an earlier work (*Non consumiamo Marx*) and the voice of Fidel Castro. The medium is

19. *...explosante-fixe...* first appeared in 'Canons and epitaphs', *Tempo*, 98 (1972), as part of a tribute to Stravinsky. Boulez describes it as a 'text to serve as a basis for proliferation'. Several pages of explanation were included, as a guide to realisation. However, Boulez was asked to make his own realisation and this has led him to present the work combining conventional instruments and live electronics.

20. Dominique Jameux and Pierre Boulez, 'Entretien. Pierre Boulez: sur *Polyphonie X* et *Poésie pour pouvoir*', *Musique en Jeu*, xvi (1974), p 33.

21. See Paul Griffiths, *A guide to electronic music*, London, 1979, p 36–41.

22. Luciano Berio, 'Poetry and Music – An Experiment', tr. John Saunders, *Prospice*, x 1979, p 10.

23. Luciano Berio, op cit, p 16.

well suited to such political expressions but it lends itself equally well to pure musical argument. For example, *Inharmonique* (1977) by Jean-Claude Risset (b. 1938) combines live soprano singing in wordless vocalise with a complex computer tape (realised at IRCAM) which ranges from pure sounds to white noise and covers the extremes of pitch.

Voices may also be modified through live electronic treatment, reverberation, tape-delay, ring-modulation, mixer techniques, etc. Using such devices, the composer may create spatial effects, adding reverberation to give the impression of a large acoustic space; creating accumulative effects by the use of tape-delay; transforming the pitch material by introducing ring-modulation or other devices – the possibilities are almost limitless. The large resources of the live electronic vocal group may further be augmented by the use of pre-composed tape. What results is truly a new genre, which brings together developments in vocal techniques and electronics. Performing groups who specialise in such music have sprung up[24] and a repertoire is quickly growing.

Concrete poetry / text–sound composition

To make a more complete picture of contemporary efforts to synthesise the media of music and poetry, it is necessary to take account of the contribution of the Concrete poets and of the text–sound composers.

The 'concrete' of Concrete poetry has little to do with the 'concrète' of Pierre Schaeffer's *musique concrète*. While Schaeffer took environmental sounds to create collages of sound derived from the real and 'concrete' world, the Concrete poets sought to create a new artistic reality – the concreteness of the artwork independent of external reality. The idea of creating an art form without reference to external reality has much in common with the ideas of the Neo-Plastic school of artists, and the connection between Concrete poetry and Neo-Plasticism is not one of mere parallelism but one of direct influence. The attitude of Concrete poets and Neo-Plastic artists to the value of non-referential art is clearly expressed by van Doesburg in these words:

If an object of experience as such enters visibly into the work, the object is an auxiliary means within the expressional means. The mode of expression will in this event be inexact.

When the aesthetic experience is expressed directly through the creative means of the branch of art in question, the mode of expression will be exact.[25]

It was this 'exactness' that Eugen Gomringer (b. 1924), the founder of the West German Concrete poetry movement, sought in

24. Two British groups who work in this medium are Singcircle, formed in 1976, and Electric Phoenix, whose debut performance took place in 1978.
25. Cited in Liselotte Gumpel, *'Concrete' poetry from East and West Germany*, New Haven, 1976.

his work. Gomringer came into close contact with the theories of Neo-Plasticism when he worked as secretary to Max Bill (b. 1908). Bill, a Swiss painter who studied at the Bauhaus and created geometrical abstractions in the style of Mondrian, was one of the Züricher Konkreten painters. When Gomringer left Bill's service in 1958, he established the Eugen Gomringer Press, for the purpose of publishing 'concrete' works.

Like Neo-Plastic art, Concrete poetry sought independence from representation. The new poetry it created was built from the word itself, using all aspects of the word – phonemes, the shapes of letters, and semantic content. Although semantic content was retained, a great reduction of this component took place. Concrete poetry thus developed a very economical use of language, subject-

avenidas
avenidas y flores

flores
flores y mujeres

avenidas
avenidas y mujeres

avenidas y flores y mujeres y
un admirador
Example 69

ing a severely limited vocabulary to the devices of repetition and juxtaposition.

The tension and ambiguity created between the three aspects of the word were essential to the working of Concrete poetry. The poem oscillates between sonic, optic and semantic spheres and acquires meaning through the various relationships thus created. A poem may create a two-way tension between the semantic and the visual, as does Gomringer's *Avenidas* (Example 69). This early poem retains a semantic bias, however, the visual component being restricted to a typographical imitation of avenues. Reinhard Döhl's *Apfel*, a 'pattern poem with an elusive intruder',[26] illustrates the semantic–visual tension more clearly (Example 70). Other Concrete poems create a three-way tension. Emmett Williams's *Cellar*

26. Emmett Williams, *An anthology of concrete poetry*, New York, 1967.

Example 70

song for five voices draws equally on all three components (Example 71). Its 120 permutations of the sentence create typographical patterns, and a certain degree of semantic content is retained, while the title tells us that the piece is to be performed as a song.

Text–sound composition is a form of Concrete poetry which exists only in sound. It may be considered as a branch of electro–

first voice: somewhere
second voice: bluebirds are flying
third voice: high in the sky.
fourth voice: in the cellar
fifth voice: even blackbirds are extinct.

```
somewhere bluebirds are flying high in the sky. in the cellar even blackbirds are extinct.
somewhere bluebirds are flying high in the sky. even blackbirds are extinct. in the cellar
somewhere bluebirds are flying in the cellar high in the sky. even blackbirds are extinct.
somewhere bluebirds are flying in the cellar even blackbirds are extinct. high in the sky.
somewhere bluebirds are flying even blackbirds are extinct. high in the sky. in the cellar
somewhere bluebirds are flying even blackbirds are extinct. in the cellar high in the sky.
somewhere high in the sky. bluebirds are flying in the cellar even blackbirds are extinct.
somewhere high in the sky. bluebirds are flying even blackbirds are extinct. in the cellar
somewhere high in the sky. in the cellar bluebirds are flying even blackbirds are extinct.
somewhere high in the sky. in the cellar even blackbirds are extinct. bluebirds are flying
somewhere high in the sky. even blackbirds are extinct. bluebirds are flying in the cellar
somewhere high in the sky. even blackbirds are extinct. in the cellar bluebirds are flying
somewhere in the cellar bluebirds are flying high in the sky. even blackbirds are extinct.
somewhere in the cellar bluebirds are flying even blackbirds are extinct. high in the sky.
somewhere in the cellar high in the sky. bluebirds are flying even blackbirds are extinct.
somewhere in the cellar high in the sky. even blackbirds are extinct. bluebirds are flying
somewhere in the cellar even blackbirds are extinct. bluebirds are flying high in the sky.
somewhere in the cellar even blackbirds are extinct. high in the sky. bluebirds are flying
somewhere even blackbirds are extinct. bluebirds are flying high in the sky. in the cellar
somewhere even blackbirds are extinct. bluebirds are flying in the cellar high in the sky.
somewhere even blackbirds are extinct. high in the sky. bluebirds are flying in the cellar
somewhere even blackbirds are extinct. high in the sky. in the cellar bluebirds are flying
somewhere even blackbirds are extinct. in the cellar bluebirds are flying high in the sky.
somewhere even blackbirds are extinct. in the cellar high in the sky. bluebirds are flying
bluebirds are flying somewhere high in the sky. even blackbirds are extinct. in the cellar
bluebirds are flying somewhere high in the sky. even blackbirds are extinct. in the cellar
bluebirds are flying somewhere in the cellar high in the sky. even blackbirds are extinct.
bluebirds are flying somewhere in the cellar even blackbirds are extinct. high in the sky.
bluebirds are flying somewhere even blackbirds are extinct. high in the sky. in the cellar
bluebirds are flying somewhere even blackbirds are extinct. in the cellar high in the sky.
bluebirds are flying high in the sky. somewhere in the cellar even blackbirds are extinct.
bluebirds are flying high in the sky. somewhere even blackbirds are extinct. in the cellar
bluebirds are flying high in the sky. in the cellar somewhere even blackbirds are extinct.
bluebirds are flying high in the sky. in the cellar even blackbirds are extinct. somewhere
bluebirds are flying high in the sky. even blackbirds are extinct. somewhere in the cellar
bluebirds are flying high in the sky. even blackbirds are extinct. in the cellar somewhere
bluebirds are flying in the cellar somewhere high in the sky. even blackbirds are extinct.
bluebirds are flying in the cellar somewhere even blackbirds are extinct. high in the sky.
bluebirds are flying in the cellar high in the sky. somewhere even blackbirds are extinct.
bluebirds are flying in the cellar high in the sky. even blackbirds are extinct. somewhere
bluebirds are flying in the cellar even blackbirds are extinct. somewhere high in the sky.
bluebirds are flying in the cellar even blackbirds are extinct. high in the sky. somewhere
bluebirds are flying even blackbirds are extinct. somewhere high in the sky. in the cellar
bluebirds are flying even blackbirds are extinct. somewhere in the cellar high in the sky.
bluebirds are flying even blackbirds are extinct. high in the sky. somewhere in the cellar
bluebirds are flying even blackbirds are extinct. high in the sky. in the cellar somewhere
bluebirds are flying even blackbirds are extinct. in the cellar somewhere high in the sky.
bluebirds are flying even blackbirds are extinct. in the cellar high in the sky. somewhere
high in the sky. somewhere bluebirds are flying in the cellar even blackbirds are extinct.
high in the sky. somewhere bluebirds are flying even blackbirds are extinct. in the cellar
high in the sky. somewhere in the cellar bluebirds are flying even blackbirds are extinct.
high in the sky. somewhere in the cellar even blackbirds are extinct. bluebirds are flying
high in the sky. somewhere even blackbirds are extinct. bluebirds are flying in the cellar
high in the sky. somewhere even blackbirds are extinct. in the cellar bluebirds are flying
high in the sky. bluebirds are flying somewhere in the cellar even blackbirds are extinct.
high in the sky. bluebirds are flying somewhere even blackbirds are extinct. in the cellar
high in the sky. bluebirds are flying in the cellar somewhere even blackbirds are extinct.
high in the sky. bluebirds are flying in the cellar even blackbirds are extinct. somewhere
high in the sky. bluebirds are flying even blackbirds are extinct. somewhere in the cellar
high in the sky. bluebirds are flying even blackbirds are extinct. in the cellar somewhere
```

Example 71

acoustic music, as it is a medium which consists of tape compositions. The difficulty of categorising text–sound composition
reflects its intermedial nature. Text–sound composition reduces the
three-way tension of sonic, optic and semantic spheres to a two-
way tension, exploring the relationship between sound and meaning – combining sonic and semantic components in different

```
high in the sky. in the cellar somewhere bluebirds are flying even blackbirds are extinct.
high in the sky. in the cellar somewhere even blackbirds are extinct. bluebirds are flying
high in the sky. in the cellar bluebirds are flying somewhere even blackbirds are extinct.
high in the sky. in the cellar bluebirds are flying even blackbirds are extinct. somewhere
high in the sky. in the cellar even blackbirds are extinct. somewhere bluebirds are flying
high in the sky. in the cellar even blackbirds are extinct. bluebirds are flying somewhere
high in the sky. even blackbirds are extinct. somewhere bluebirds are flying in the cellar
high in the sky. even blackbirds are extinct. somewhere in the cellar bluebirds are flying
high in the sky. even blackbirds are extinct. bluebirds are flying somewhere in the cellar
high in the sky. even blackbirds are extinct. bluebirds are flying in the cellar somewhere
high in the sky. even blackbirds are extinct. in the cellar somewhere bluebirds are flying
high in the sky. even blackbirds are extinct. in the cellar bluebirds are flying somewhere
in the cellar somewhere bluebirds are flying high in the sky. even blackbirds are extinct.
in the cellar somewhere bluebirds are flying even blackbirds are extinct. high in the sky.
in the cellar somewhere high in the sky. bluebirds are flying even blackbirds are extinct.
in the cellar somewhere high in the sky. even blackbirds are extinct. bluebirds are flying
in the cellar somewhere even blackbirds are extinct. bluebirds are flying high in the sky.
in the cellar somewhere even blackbirds are extinct. high in the sky bluebirds are flying.
in the cellar bluebirds are flying somewhere high in the sky. even blackbirds are extinct.
in the cellar bluebirds are flying somewhere even blackbirds are extinct. high in the sky.
in the cellar bluebirds are flying high in the sky. somewhere even blackbirds are extinct.
in the cellar bluebirds are flying high in the sky. even blackbirds are extinct. somewhere
in the cellar bluebirds are flying even blackbirds are extinct. somewhere high in the sky.
in the cellar bluebirds are flying even blackbirds are extinct. high in the sky. somewhere
in the cellar high in the sky. somewhere bluebirds are flying even blackbirds are extinct.
in the cellar high in the sky. somewhere even blackbirds are extinct. bluebirds are flying
in the cellar high in the sky. bluebirds are flying somewhere even blackbirds are extinct.
in the cellar high in the sky. bluebirds are flying even blackbirds are extinct. somewhere
in the cellar high in the sky. even blackbirds are extinct. somewhere bluebirds are flying
in the cellar high in the sky. even blackbirds are extinct. bluebirds are flying somewhere
in the cellar even blackbirds are extinct. somewhere bluebirds are flying high in the sky.
in the cellar even blackbirds are extinct. somewhere high in the sky. bluebirds are flying
in the cellar even blackbirds are extinct. bluebirds are flying somewhere high in the sky.
in the cellar even blackbirds are extinct. bluebirds are flying high in the sky. somewhere
in the cellar even blackbirds are extinct. high in the sky. somewhere bluebirds are flying
in the cellar even blackbirds are extinct. high in the sky. bluebirds are flying somewhere
even blackbirds are extinct. somewhere bluebirds are flying high in the sky. in the cellar
even blackbirds are extinct. somewhere bluebirds are flying in the cellar high in the sky.
even blackbirds are extinct. somewhere high in the sky. bluebirds are flying in the cellar
even blackbirds are extinct. somewhere high in the sky. in the cellar bluebirds are flying
even blackbirds are extinct. somewhere in the cellar bluebirds are flying high in the sky.
even blackbirds are extinct. somewhere in the cellar high in the sky. bluebirds are flying
even blackbirds are extinct. bluebirds are flying somewhere high in the sky. in the cellar
even blackbirds are extinct. bluebirds are flying somewhere in the cellar high in the sky.
even blackbirds are extinct. bluebirds are flying high in the sky. somewhere in the cellar
even blackbirds are extinct. bluebirds are flying high in the sky. in the cellar somewhere
even blackbirds are extinct. bluebirds are flying in the cellar somewhere high in the sky.
even blackbirds are extinct. bluebirds are flying in the cellar high in the sky. somewhere
even blackbirds are extinct. high in the sky. somewhere bluebirds are flying in the cellar
even blackbirds are extinct. high in the sky. somewhere in the cellar bluebirds are flying
even blackbirds are extinct. high in the sky. bluebirds are flying somewhere in the cellar
even blackbirds are extinct. high in the sky. bluebirds are flying in the cellar somewhere
even blackbirds are extinct. high in the sky. in the cellar somewhere bluebirds are flying
even blackbirds are extinct. high in the sky. in the cellar bluebirds are flying somewhere
even blackbirds are extinct. in the cellar somewhere bluebirds are flying high in the sky.
even blackbirds are extinct. in the cellar somewhere high in the sky. bluebirds are flying
even blackbirds are extinct. in the cellar bluebirds are flying somewhere high in the sky.
even blackbirds are extinct. in the cellar bluebirds are flying high in the sky. somewhere
even blackbirds are extinct. in the cellar high in the sky. somewhere bluebirds are flying
even blackbirds are extinct. in the cellar high in the sky. bluebirds are flying somewhere
```

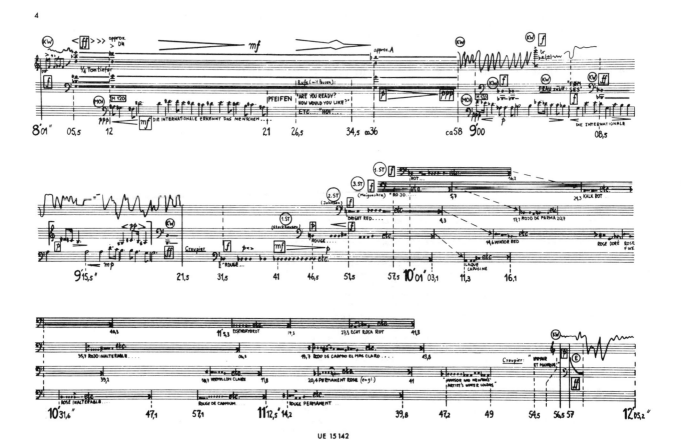

Example 72

proportions. Because text–sound composition exists in time, it is possible for the proportions of semantic and sonic components to change during the course of the piece. Steve Reich's *Come out* opens with the recorded words of David Hamm, one of six boys on trial for murder after the 1964 Harlem riots: 'I had to like open the bruise up to let the bruise blood come out to show them'.[27] The sentence has semantic content and carries a certain contextual significance. Later in the piece, sound patterns are generated from a tape loop of the words 'come out to show them' and the semantic component is substantially reduced. Stockhausen's text–sound episode in the First Region of *Hymnen* (a piece using the national anthems of many countries of the world) is more static, its semantic component remaining at a constant level in its polylingual reiteration of the word red – the colour symbolising the socialist anthem (Example 72).

The objectives of the Concrete poets and of Boulez were similar. Both intended to create an autonomous artistic language and, in this, both were influenced by the principles of Neo-Plasticism. It is quite remarkable to discover that movements sharing the same parentage could achieve such dramatically different results. Boulez

27. The boys were being taken to be 'cleaned up' by the police. As Hamm had no external bleeding, he squeezed a bruise until it bled.

was influenced by the rigour of Neo-Plastic art to create a musical language that was self-sufficient and made no reference to foregoing principles of organisation.[28] Thus, he developed systems for the organisation and interaction of the musical parameters. However, his expression remained within the defining bounds of the medium. He may have sought in poetry for an 'irrigation' of music or for musical equivalents of poetic models, but the resultant art form remained securely within music's defining limits. By contrast, Concrete poetry applied the principles of Neo-Plasticism to the question of referentiality in poetry, and what resulted was a truly intermedial form. One constantly wonders – is this music or poetry? This question is resolved in a realisation that it is both, that the expression has broken the boundaries which defined the media. The poet need no longer 'put music before everything' and idolise music as Verlaine did; instead he can enter directly into an expression which unites the media.

The influence of Neo-Plastic theories on referential media was to cause a referential system to be replaced by a systematic one. In the case of art, representation was replaced by geometrical expression. In poetry, it meant the abandonment, or reduction, of the semantic component and its replacement by a systematic arrangement, exploiting visual, sonic and semantic aspects of the word. But music, as a primarily systematic medium, could not be influenced in this way. Music has no representational or semantic crutch which could be replaced by some other system of organisation. However, it could be argued that the crutch which music abandoned was the crutch of traditional harmony, but the substitution of serial techniques for tonal ones resulted simply in the substitution of one autonomous system for another.

28. With the important exception of the Second Viennese School, Messiaen and Stravinsky, whose influence has been discussed in Chapter I.

VI · From Avant-Garde to Mainstream

At the first opportunity there was a break-out from the
stifling prison of *number*, and then EVERYTHING was
allowed including the most idiotic and vulgar
exhibitionism. Did anyone expect thus to escape the only
reality? And what did this general permissiveness and
these long holidays from thought signify, if not a
continued flight from responsibility?

Boulez, 1960[1]

When Boulez began his career as a composer, his music was truly
revolutionary and the polemical position he adopted to support his
position clearly merited the military appellation 'avant-garde'.
Boulez stood at the head of a movement which swept aside the
traditional principles of musical organisation and established a new
and uncompromising language. Contemporary commentators
were flabbergasted:

What are we to make of a work like Boulez's *Le marteau sans maître*. . .which did
full justice to its title by hammering away mercilessly for over half an hour. . .?[2]

Other commentators made more specific criticisms. Harold Rutland, for example, bemoaned the passing of the 'memorable theme'.

With Boulez. . .we reach a bankruptcy of thematic invention. Texture is all, jagged
intervals such as ninths and augmented octaves abound, rhythms are consistently
irregular, and the whole thing is spasmodic, moving by fits and starts, (is it 'all
done by mathematics'?).

. . .*Le marteau* lasts for some thirty-five minutes, and I know I am not alone in
feeling that with so little for the ear to fasten on, the music ends, after the novelty
has worn off, by becoming exasperating and a bore.[3]

But Boulez's position as *enfant terrible* was not to last.
Experimental music took the stage and the musical scene diversi-
fied. Experimental music is seen today as a movement in many
respects distinct from the avant-garde movement.[4] While avant-
garde music is a development of European traditions (tracing its
heritage through Webern, Schoenberg, Mahler, Wagner and back to
J. S. Bach), experimental music was largely a North American
movement, with no such distinguished parentage. It was not
conceived as art-music, and it opposed the idea of art as a com-

1. Pierre Boulez, *O.M.T.*, p 26.
2. Franz Reizenstein, 'I.S.C.M. Festival
at Baden-Baden', *Musical Times* ivc
(1955), p 437.
3. Harold Rutland, 'The new music',
Musical Times, ci (1960), p 233.
4. The distinction between the movements is clearly drawn by Michael
Nyman, *Experimental music: Cage and
beyond*, New York, 1974.

modity. Boulez's position in new music has now developed to a point where he has acquired the status of a classic avant-garde composer and can be described as typifying an art that is 'well-established, central, mainstream. . .'.[5]

From the outset, Boulez's objective had been to establish a new language of music and, having been a crucial figure in the development of a 'lingua franca' of new music, he has adhered to his position and condemned any departures in most certain terms. One of the most remarkable features of Boulez the composer is his adherence to his aesthetic objectives and loyalty to the artists who influenced the formation of those objectives. This does not mean that his compositional technique has remained unchanged, but that any development has been a controlled and carefully thought-out extension of the original premises.[6] Nor does it mean that he has not been influenced by contemporary developments, for he has incorporated chance elements into his works and begun to explore the element of space (in *Domaines*, for example), but any such feature is always carefully integrated into his compositional technique and made to conform to the 'new logic of sound-relationships'.[7]

Boulez has remained true to the artists and musicians who influenced him so strongly as a young man; the aesthetic basis of his art is unchanged. In the matter of the relationship of music and text, Boulez has remained similarly loyal to his early ideas. He has not been lured by the siren-songs of music–theatre, nor has he been tempted to enter the realms of the paralinguistic. His focus has remained securely on the relationship of music and poetry, their formal interaction, and the creation of equivalents of one for the other. And this continued, detailed and sophisticated exploration of poetry as an irrigation of music is one of the most distinguishing features of his contribution as a composer.

5. Reginald Smith Brindle, *The new music*, London, 1975, p 133.
6. For a brief but lucid description of Boulez's development of the serial principle, see Paul Griffiths, *Boulez*, London, 1978.
7. Pierre Boulez, *O.M.T.*, p 25.

List of principal works

Boulez's approach to composition causes problems for the tidy-minded musicologist who would like to attribute *definitive* dates to his works. Boulez frequently revises works, he 'never completely detaches himself from a work'. Moreover, he is occasionally moved to withdraw a work completely. It becomes difficult, therefore, to know which work should be included in a list, let alone the date to be attributed to it. The following is a list of principal works: it ignores juvenilia and incidental music for film or theatre.

DATE OF COMPOSITION		WORK	INSTRUMENTATION	PUBLISHER AND COPYRIGHT DATE	STATUS
1945		*Notations*	piano		withdrawn
	1978		large orchestra	Universal	
1946		*Sonatine*	flute and piano	Amphion 1954	
		Piano sonata no. 1	piano	Amphion 1951	
1946–47		*Le visage nuptial*	(1st version) soprano, contralto, two *ondes martenot*, piano, percussion		
	1951–52		(2nd version) soprano, contralto, female chorus, orchestra	Heugel 1959	
1947–48		Piano sonata No. 2	piano	Heugel 1950	
1948		*Le soleil des eaux*	(1st version) voices and orchestra		withdrawn
	1950		(2nd version) soprano, tenor, bass and orchestra		withdrawn
	1958		(3rd version) soprano, tenor, bass, STB chorus and orchestra	Heugel 1959	
	1965		(4th version) soprano, SATB chorus and orchestra	Heugel 1968	
1948–49		*Livre pour quatuor*	string quartet	Heugel 1960 (omitting IV and VI)	withdrawn
	1968	revised as *Livre pour cordes*	string orchestra		
1951		*Polyphonie X*	eighteen instruments		withdrawn, revision in progress
1951/1952		*Étude sur un son*	single track tape		
		Étude sur sept sons	single track tape		
		Structures, Livre I	two pianos	Universal 1955	
1952		*Oubli signal lapidé* (text by Gatti)	twelve voices		withdrawn
1953–55		*Le marteau sans maître*	contralto, alto flute, xylorimba, vibraphone, percussion, guitar, viola	Universal 1954	
	1957	*Le marteau* revision		Universal 1957 Philharmonia 1976	
1956–57		Piano sonata no. 3	piano		
		Antiphonie		Universal 1968	
		Trope		Universal 1961	
		Constellation		Universal 1963	
		Strophe			revision in progress
		Séquence			revision in progress

DATE OF COMPOSITION	WORK	INSTRUMENTATION	PUBLISHER AND COPYRIGHT DATE	STATUS
1956–61	*Structures, Livre II*	two pianos	Universal 1967	
1957–62	*Pli selon pli*			
1957	*Improvisation sur Mallarmé I*	soprano, harp, vibraphone, tubular bells, and four percussion	Universal 1958	
1962	*Improvisation sur Mallarmé I*	(alternative version) soprano and small orchestra	Universal 1977	
1957	*Improvisation sur Mallarmé II*	soprano, harp, vibraphone, piano, celesta, tubular bells and four percussion	Universal 1958	
1959	*Improvisation sur Mallarmé III*	soprano and small orchestra	Universal 1971	
1959–62	*Tombeau*	soprano and orchestra	Universal 1971	
1960	*Don*	(first version) soprano and piano		withdrawn
1962		(second version) soprano and orchestra	Universal 1967	
1957–58	*Doubles*	large orchestra		
1963	revised as *Figures–doubles–prismes*			
1968	new section added			
1958	*Poésie pour pouvoir*	five-track tape and orchestra		withdrawn
1961–68	*Domaines*	clarinet solo, or with twenty-one instruments in six groups		
1980–81	revision	mixed choir, chamber choir, large orchestra and electronic equipment	Universal	
	revision		(Universal 1970, clarinet solo)	
1962–64	*Marges*	percussion ensemble		withdrawn
1965	*Eclat*	nine percussion and six instruments	Universal 1965	
1966–	revised as *Eclat-multiples*	nine percussion and orchestra	Universal	
1970	*cummings ist der dichter*	chamber chorus and orchestra	Universal 1967	
1971	*. . .explosante fixe. . .*	for variable forces	Universal 1971 in *Tempo* magazine	
1974–75	*Rituel*	orchestra in eight groups	Universal 1975	
1976	*Messagesquisse*	solo 'cello and six other 'cellos	Universal	
1981–	*Répons*	six soloists, chamber group, computer tape and live electronics	Universal	
1984	*Dérive*	chamber group	Universal	

Selective bibliography

This bibliography is not comprehensive. For further references see Michael Fink's bibliography, listed under 'Articles on Boulez', and the *Festschrift Pierre Boulez* described below.

1 *Writings by Boulez*

Boulez has written quite extensively on aesthetic and technical musical matters. Many of his articles have been collected in *Relevés d'apprenti*, translated into English as *Notes of an apprenticeship*.

(a) *Books*

Orientations: collected writings, London, Faber, 1986. Edited by Jean-Jacques Nattier and translated into English by Martin Cooper

Par volonté et par hasard: entretiens avec Célestin Deliège, Paris, Seuil, 1975. Translated into English by Robert Wangermée as *Conversations with Célestin Deliège*, London, Eulenberg, 1976

Penser la musique aujourd'hui, Paris, Gonthier, 1963. Translated into English by Susan Bradshaw and Richard Rodney Bennett as *Boulez on music today*, London, Faber, 1971

Relevés d'apprenti, Paris, Seuil, 1966. Translated into English by Herbert Weinstock as *Notes of an apprenticeship*, New York, Knopf, 1968

(b) *Articles*

'Frozen perfection', *Music and Musicians*, xvi (February 1968), 30f

'La musique: expérience, autruches et musique', *La Nouvelle Revue Française*, iii (1955), 1174–76

'Nécessité d'une orientation esthétique', *Mercure de France*, cccl (1964), 624–39, and cccli (1964), 110–22

'Poésie – centre et absence – musique', *Melos*, xxx (February 1963), 33–46

'Probabilités critiques du compositeur', *Domaine Musicale*, i (1954), 3–13

'Sonate, que me veux-tu?', translated into English by David Noakes and Paul Jacobs, *Perspectives of New Music*, i, 2 (1963), 32–44

'Sprechen, singen, spielen', *Melos*, xxxviii (November 1971), 453–60

'Technology and the composer', *Times Literary Supplement* (6 May 1977), 570–71

2 *Monographs on Boulez*

Goléa, Antoine, *Recontres avec Pierre Boulez*, Paris, 1958
Griffiths, Paul, *Boulez*, London, 1978
Jameux, Dominique, *Pierre Boulez*, Paris, 1984
Peyser, Joan, *Boulez: composer, conductor, enigma*, London, 1977

3 *Books discussing Boulez among others*

Barraud, Henry, *Pour comprendre les musiques d'aujourd'hui*, Paris, 1968
Brindle, Reginald Smith, *The new music*, London, 1975
Griffiths, Paul, *A concise history of modern music from Debussy to Boulez*, London, 1978
  A guide to electronic music, London, 1979
Samuel, Claude, *Panorama de l'art musical contemporain*, Paris, 1962
Whittall, Arnold, *Music since the First World War*, London, 1977

4 *Articles on Boulez*

Bradshaw, Susan and Bennett, Richard Rodney, 'In search of Boulez', *Music and Musicians*, xi (January 1963), 10–13, and (August 1963), 14–18
Cage, John, 'Four musicians at work', *trans/formation*, i, 3 (1952), 168ff
Charles, Daniel, 'Entr'acte: "formal" or "informal" music?', *The Musical Quarterly*, li (January 1965), 144–65
Cowell, Henry, 'Current chronicle', *The Musical Quarterly*, xxxviii (January 1952), 132–34
Craft, Robert, 'Boulez and Stockhausen', *Score*, xxiv (November 1958), 5462
Cross, Anthony, 'Form and expression in Boulez's *Don*', *Music Review*, xxxvi (August 1975), 215–30
  'The significance of Aleatorism in twentieth-century music', *Music Review*, xxix (1968), 305–22
Derrien, Jean–Pierre, 'Dossier: Pierre Boulez', *Musique en Jeu*, i (November 1970), 103–32
Fink, Michael, 'Pierre Boulez: a selective bibliography', *Current Musicology*, xiii (1972), 135–50
Goehr, Alexander, 'An answer to Pierre Boulez', *Times Literary Supplement* (10 June 1977), 73
Goléa, Antoine, 'French music since 1945', *The Musical Quarterly*, li (January 1965), 22–37
  'Pierre Boulez dans la musique de notre temps', *Revue Musicale*, ccxlii (1958), 49–50
Gould, Glenn, 'The dodecacophonist's dilemma', *Canadian Music Journal*, i (Autumn 1956), 63–64
Heyworth, Peter, 'The sound of Boulez', *Observer*, (3 October 1971), 29
Hopkins, G. W., 'Debussy and Boulez', *Musical Times*, cix (August 1968), 710–14
  'Boulez', *New Grove dictionary of music and musicians*
Ligeti, György, 'A propos de la *Troisième Sonate* de Boulez', *Musique en Jeu*, xvi (November 1974), 6–8
  'Pierre Boulez: decision and automation in *Structures 1a*', *Die Reihe*, iv, English edition (1960), 36–62

Northcott, Bayan, 'Boulez's theory of composition', *Music and Musicians*, xx (December 1971), 32–36

Peck, Agnes, 'Parole, silence et musique: René Char et Pierre Boulez', *Musique en Jeu*, v (November 1971), 138–40

Philippot, Michel P., 'Pierre Boulez today', *Perspectives of New Music*, v (Fall–Winter 1966), 153–60

Rimmer, Frederick, 'Sequence and symmetry in twentieth-century music', *Music Review*, xxvi (1965), 28–96

Stoianowa Iwanka, 'La Troisième Sonate de Pierre Boulez et le projet Mallarméen du Livre', *Musique en Jeu*, xvi (November 1974), 9–28

' "Pli selon pli". Portrait de Mallarmé', *Musique en Jeu*, xi (June 1973), 74–98

'Verbe et son "centre et absence" ', *Musique en Jeu*, xvi (November 1974), 79–102

Stockhausen, Karlheinz, 'Music and Speech', *Die Reihe*, vi (1964), 40–64

Whittall, Arnold, 'After Webern, Wagner. Reflections on the past and future of Pierre Boulez', *Music Review*, xxxviii (1967), 135–38

5 Symposia

Glock, William, ed. *Pierre Boulez: A Symposium*, London, Eulenburg, 1986. Articles by Gerald Bennett, Susan Bradshaw, Célestin Deliège, William Glock and Jonathan Harvey

Häusler, Josef, ed. *Pierre Boulez: Eine Festschrift zum 60. Geburtstag am 26. März 1985*, Vienna, 1985

This useful volume published on the occasion of Boulez's sixtieth birthday contains articles in English, French, and German by Elliott Carter, Ernest Fleischmann, William Glock, Clytus Gottwald, Paul Griffiths, Josef Häusler, Dominique Jameux, Hans Mayer, Lawrence Morton, Robert Piencikowski, Hans Oesch, Paul Sacher, Manfred Stahnke, and Wolfgang Wagner. It also contains a most valuable and informative section including a factual biography, a comprehensive list of works, a bibliography of Boulez's writings, a discography, and a list of films about Boulez's work as composer and conductor.

Index